GUIDE TO
Business
Law

W. MICHAEL GOUGH
DE ANZA COLLEGE

KENDALL/HUNT PUBLISHING COMPANY
4050 Westmark Drive   Dubuque, Iowa 52002

Guide to Business Law

Contents

W. Michael Gough, 2002

Chapter 1

Law Overview and Legal History

"Law is order, and good law is good order." Aristotle

Norms of Behavior

Law is defined in one dictionary as "all the rules of conduct established by the authority or custom of a nation." As a practical matter you may likely think of law as a given set of rules you have to follow in society. So in a simple sense law tells us what we can and cannot do.

Law is as old as society. Whenever people live together in a group, certain standards of behavior are adopted for the good working of the group. These standards of behavior are called norms, (normal behavior), by some. Initially, when a society is getting started the norms are informal. For example, you might have a small group of individuals you camp with every year. When the group is small everyone in the group may implicitly or explicitly understand the expectations of the group. You might have one rule where everyone is expected to quiet down by 10PM, and another where everyone is expected to share in clean up after the meals. When the group is small and everyone knows one another well, these informal norms will probably be effective in keeping the camping trip manageable.

Now suppose that the trip grows in popularity and friends of friends begin joining the trip and as the group grows so do problems. Some of the new people tend to stay noisy past 10PM. Others do not share proportionately in the work. Someone from the original small group might confront the "norm breakers" and explain to the new campers that they are breaking the "rules." As you might imagine, some of the rule breakers may say "What rules? No one ever showed us rules." At this point, you would probably decide that if the trip is to continue in the future that certain basic rules should be written down and conveyed to everyone in the group. Thus, those informal norms of behavior would have to become formalized. This in effect is how law comes about in society. At some point as a group grows, norms of behavior must be formalized so everyone knows what the rules are and how they are followed. Recognize that informal norms will still remain when formal rules or law is put forth (promulgated) for the group. For instance, there may be a formal rule about being in tents by 10PM, but no formal rule about swearing in the camp. Nevertheless, swearing might not be tolerated, despite a lack of formal rules to the contrary.

How do norms of behavior get enforced in a group? The simple answer is with sanctions. Sanctions are a means of enforcing a judgment. They are the things that give law its teeth. For example, when you are caught exceeding the speed limit in your car, you have to pay a traffic fine; and you may endure other sanctions as well such as a loss of license and so forth. If a family member stays out past curfew, she may lose the right to go out the following weekend for violating the rule.

We begin by looking at a brief history of law and tracing some of the steps of earlier societies to help give us perspective of our own.

Early Societies

It is clear that the earliest societies had rules of conduct, which were passed on and modified from generation to generation. As a society advanced and developed a written language, the writing or codifying of law was the next logical step in the society's development. The code of Hammurabi written approximately 5000 years ago in ancient Babylon and is one of the earliest examples of a society promulgating law in a written form.

The two earliest societies that had the most influence on modern day American law are the Jewish and Roman societies. It is thought that Jewish law with the Mosaic Code (from the prophet, Moses) began around 1500 BC and was expanded and refined for years thereafter. Jewish law, (like many early society's law), was tied closely to religion. The Old Testament is a mixture of religious and societal law that governed members of the Jewish State. The first five books of the Old Testament, called the *Torah,* set forth the basic law of the Jewish people. As you are probably aware, the most important part of the Old Testament is the Ten Commandments. Consider some of the Ten Commandments and you will see that many of the commandments do a good job of establishing reasonable behavior in society. "Thou shalt not kill; steal; covet another's spouse," are good recommendations for living peacefully with others in any group. The *Torah* was expanded upon in the *Talmud,* which codified law to a much greater degree than in the *Torah* and influenced Roman law as it came into existence.

Roman Law

Roman law had a profound influence on modern day law throughout the western world. The Romans produced their first known code of law around 450 BC, called the *Code of Twelve Tables.* As the empire progressed, so too did the law system. Through the years a set of legal principles developed that governed all people who fell under Roman rule. This set of principles was called the *jus gentium* (law of nations). The *jus gentium* was based on the notions of justice and fairness while taking local customs and practices into account.

The Romans also developed a comprehensive set of codes that detailed the laws set forth in the *Code of Twelve Tables* called *Corpus Juris Civillis* (Body of Civil Law). This written law that expanded on the basic law developed in the *Code of Twelve Tables* is similar to statutory law (written law) in present day society. The civil law was divided into civil (private) and criminal (public) matters. A civil offense was one where you might sue a neighbor or business because of a contract violation. A criminal offense was one where the society would take action against you in a murder or theft case.

The Romans were advanced enough to have negligence laws. This is an area we will study later in the course, but simply put, the Romans were able to govern actions of individuals in such a way that you could be liable for not being careful enough when going about your daily business. For instance, if you did not maintain your ox cart and a wheel came off injuring another, you could be held liable for damages. This serves as an example of the importance of vehicle maintenance even in the first century.

In the Roman system, judges were not empowered to make law where it did not exist. Their primary function was to decide which party had a majority of the evidence on his side and rule accordingly. This is in contrast to the common law system where judges can actually make law in certain cases, which is part of the system of laws we follow in the United States.

As advanced as Roman society was, it began to decline around 200 AD when Rome could not continue to hold the empire together. The Roman Empire was invaded by the Goths, (Germanic Tribes), and Persians between 200 and 400 AD. The decline of Rome was complete by 470 AD but its systems of laws influenced law systems throughout the western world to the present day.

Middle Ages and Feudalism

The Middle Ages, also known as the Dark Ages, took place after the fall of Rome. Once Rome fell there was no clear central government as had been the case during the Roman Empire. The Germanic tribes that had defeated the Western portion of the Roman Empire divided the lands into many kingdoms, which fell under separate tribal chiefs. The Germanic peoples, called barbarians by the Romans, were loyal to their tribal chiefs and their families. Barbarian custom began to replace Roman law at that point.

Feudalism is associated with the Middle Ages and Charlemagne is credited with being the key figure in its institution. During Charlemagne's rule all property was considered to belong to the king. He had the right to parcel out the property to noblemen who in return were expected to support him in all ways. The nobleman would then parcel out lesser parcels to lesser nobles who ultimately rented the property to serfs who paid rent by giving over a large portion of the crops they would farm on the land. Thus, the nobleman collected the fee from the estate. The concept of real property came into being at this time.

Disputes during this period were settled somewhat differently than in Roman times. When there was a dispute between two vassals (two noblemen), the lord or king would preside over the proceedings much like a judge does today. The other vassals, (noblemen who were social peers much like today's jury), would decide the case and present judgment on the two involved in the dispute.

A vassal had a duty to answer a summons (an order to appear) at the feudal court. If the vassal did not appear or did not obey the court's decision the lord could take back the vassal's land (or fief). A rebellious vassal was labeled a felon.

English Law - Common Law Beginnings

1066 is the date we associate with William the Conqueror and the Norman Conquest of England. The Normans had a system of travelling courts that were empowered to settle disputes between litigants. Because there was no central government as there had been in Rome centuries before, and because courts on the mainland of Europe settled disputes locally, these travelling courts settled disputes of the common man based on the judges sense of law, justice and precedent. If a case before the court was a 'new case', one that had never been seen before; the judge decided what law should apply and made his decision. This decision would set a precedent that could be utilized later by courts with similar issues that came up. Thus the term, "stare decisis" meaning stand by the (earlier) decision came into being in England. This "judge made" law is referred to as common law and became one of the cornerstones of English law.

The king of England still held power and his word was law in England. He made law (written law that we call statutory law) that had to be followed by people and courts alike. But the English monarchs did not crank out law like the Romans did; rather the English empowered the courts to make common law in settling disputes.

There were some in Europe who believed in a concept called the "divine right of kings"; meaning that the king was effectively chosen by God and that only God could punish a king. In some circles it was believed that disobeying the king was the same as disobeying God. The Christian religion with its promise of an afterlife had a fast hold on most of the populace in Europe at the time.

One issue that came to fore in England was that the courts were somewhat inflexible in the remedies that could be granted to a litigant. The English kings allowed courts of law two possible remedies. Basically, a court could jail someone or force him or her to pay a fine or damages. This remedy would be of little help to you if you wished to have someone stop trespassing on your land or if you wanted to force someone to deliver goods that you had contracted and paid for. To get these types of remedies you had to present your case to the king who had the ultimate power over his subjects. The king delegated this duty to a Lord Chancellor, usually a learned high churchman who was referred to as the "conscience of the king." He was empowered to grant a remedy other than the traditional remedies that courts of law provided. This was the beginning of courts of equity in England. Equity courts were granted the power to provide remedies other than those available at law.

A third court developed in addition to the law courts and equity courts was the merchant court. This was a specialized court developed to deal with merchants who sold goods travelling around England and Europe during the Middle Ages. This court was set up deal with their commercial disputes. So even then there was recognition that a special set of laws was in order for business people plying their trade. An outgrowth of this is the Uniform Commercial Code in the United States that has been in existence since the 19th century.

For over a hundred years starting in 1066, able kings ruled England and followed the rules of feudal law. There was no check on the king's power, but the English kings governed justly for the most part. In 1199, King John ascended the throne in England and abused his power from the outset of his reign. He demanded more military service than required under feudalism. He forced common law courts to accede to his wishes instead of following common law, and he taxed the populace at an unfair, high rate. In 1215 AD, many of the noble class forced John to sign the *Magna Carta* which limited the power of the king and required the king to recognize what was a constitutional check on his power. Though the *Magna Carta* was written primarily for the noble class, it was a document that would ultimately influence the American government over half a millenium later with the idea that a class of people should be self governed and that the ruler would have limits to his power. This was quite a departure from the idea of the divine right of kings.

From the Middle Ages through the Renaissance, the common law system of England was refined. England, like other strong European nations began exploring and colonizing countries far from Europe. As we can attest from our English language, England was successful in colonizing what is now the United States. The settlers from England brought the system of common law with them and established it as our system of courts and laws. This is in contrast to other European nations that utilized the Roman, Civil law system that we now see in France, Spain and other European countries.

We refined the system of common law to suit our nation's needs so we have some differences from the English system, but the basic approach of both systems is the same.

American Law

After the Revolutionary War, Americans faced a dilemma. Our citizenry was distrustful of a strong central government. The colonies were now a group of loosely aligned states that needed some type of central government to unite the country and provide for defense against other nations. However, the citizens had no interest in a dictator or any type central ruler who had few checks on his or her power. The U.S. Constitution resolved this issue by forming a government made up of three separate, equal branches. The three branches have to work together and are forced to compromise on contentious issues, which keeps any one branch from assuming more power than another.

In the first century after the Revolutionary War the United States was an agricultural economy. Most of our citizens lived on or around farms. The average individual in the US grew up, worked and died in a small agricultural village or town. Consequently, if you lived during that time, you knew most of the people in your small society and informal norms helped protect you from unscrupulous business people. If the general store owner took advantage of a child in the village, a parent would likely march back to the store and chastise the owner for his actions. Informal norms work well in a small society. Those of you who attended small schools when you were younger know the workings of a small society and the force of informal norms of behavior. At that time the prevailing theory of government was that of "the government that governs least governs best." The term "laissez faire", meaning "hands off" was the philosophy of government. Consequently, the government was not a burden on its citizens but nor was it of much protection for its citizens.

Toward the end of the 19th century, our society began to "spread out." The industrial revolution was taking hold and individuals were leaving the farm for opportunities in the city. The transcontinental railroad had been built and now instead of buying all of your goods from a savvy general store owner who made quarterly shopping trips to the big city; you could buy goods directly from mail order merchants (think of those two entrepreneurs - Sears and Roebuck). What could you do if you lived in Sacramento, CA and you purchased an item from a mail order house in Chicago IL, and the store sent the wrong item? What were your rights? Would a laissez faire approach by the government help you?

As you might imagine, citizens began telling our legislators that there was a need for more government protection in the business place. That idea was particularly brought to light when tainted meat was sold at the turn of the 20th century in New York City, and people died as a result of that scandal. More became expected of the government and so federal and state governments legislated much more consumer protection and began expanding regulation by instituting administrative agencies like the Federal Trade Commission and the Food and Drug Administration. The government became less "hands off" and more "hands on."

The 20th and 21st centuries have seen extraordinary growth in the rise of consumer protection and administrative agencies. There is much more government regulation in the marketplace and in our lives than ever before. This is in stark contrast to our approach than two hundred years ago when the populace feared a strong central government and advocated a laissez faire philosophy.

Chapter 2

Legal Philosophy

"Circumstances alter cases" - Thomas Chandler Haliburton

Most of us have an understanding of how law is made. At the federal level the senate and House of Representatives agree on a bill, send it to the president and it is signed into law. The president issues an executive order. A judge makes a common law decision. While we understand how law is made, a more difficult question is why is law made. What underlying reasons do we have for passing certain laws?

For example, prior to 1972, abortion was illegal in the United States. After that time it has been legal. Most of us know this was a common law decision made by the United States Supreme Court. We are also aware that it is a contentious issue that generates strong feelings on both sides, but why was the law made? What was the underlying philosophy in that law and other laws that are passed?

Philosophers have been attempting to answer those questions for centuries. Understanding how experts view the underlying reasons for law can be helpful in understanding the law and its sources. As is always the case, historical perspective can be helpful in explaining in a broad sense how a nation might view government and the law.

The Individual and Societal Ethic

A crucial theory that was subscribed to in the U.S. for the first 120 years or so after winning our freedom from England is that the government is best that governs least. The French term *'laissez faire'* - means hands off and some described our form of government that way. There was a strong belief in what is known as the individual ethic. The government stayed out of your business and your life to a great degree and left you to your own devices. This also meant that if you had bad luck and had trouble making a living the government left you to your own devices as well. This could be very harsh if you were born poor and signed a contract to work in a dangerous coal mine that did not pay you enough to pay for your rent and food. But, by the same token, if you were industrious and able to start a successful business, the government did little, if anything, to interfere with the way you ran your business. In the 1800's the saying "a deal is a deal" originated meaning if you made a good, bad or indifferent contract, you would be held to it. It was not the government's job to protect you or to weigh you down. As a matter of fact, it was often said in the halls of congress during the 19th century that it was not the government's job to "protect a fool and his money." Thus the idea that an individual is free to make his or her own choices and live with the consequences - the individual ethic was the prevailing theory of the time.

The individual ethic is contrasted with the societal ethic where the underlying theory is that the individual gives up rights for the common good. In the mid 19th century Karl Marx articulated the idea of a societal ethic to an extreme with his ideas in *Das Kapital*, which advocated communism. This ethic followed the thinking of "from each individual according to his ability, to each individual according to his need." The United States followed the individual ethic strongly through the 19th century. In the 20th century we began to move toward a societal ethic, where some individual rights are given up for the common good. An example of how our country changed its thinking in this regard is the union movement in America. Prior to the 1920's groups of workers tried unsuccessfully to bargain with business owners and require them to pay a living wage, institute safety policies in companies, and negotiate in good faith with elected workers of unions. Owners refused to do so and were backed up by the courts. In the 1920's and 1930's laws were instituted and upheld allowing workers to unionize and forcing owners to recognize unions and negotiate with them. The owners were forced to give up an individual right in this example for the common good. Another example of how we have moved toward the societal ethic is in private property ownership. We have national and state parks owned by the government that individuals cannot own so the whole of society can enjoy these lands. In an absolute free market economy all property is owned by individuals or private parties. So we can surmise that while we are a free nation with strong individual rights, we have moved farther along toward the societal ethic and away from the individual ethic.

Legal Philosophers

While there is no shortage of philosophers or learned individuals with opinions on legal theory, there are a few that are worth becoming familiar with in a Business Law course.

Below are some philosophers and a brief explanation of their theories that may help explain how law and human behavior come together:

Aristotle - Divine or Natural Law

Aristotle believed that humans are born with an innate sense of what is right and wrong, good and evil. He believed that the only laws that should be carried out are those that are good, just laws. Those laws that are evil are not law in divine or natural law. An historical example of a law that most would consider wrong or evil was the legality of slavery in the United States. This would be considered a law that is not true law because it does not treat all individuals equally and most would contend it is fundamentally immoral. Aristotle believed that true law is tied to moral behavior.

Roscoe Pound - Social Engineering

Pound was a legal scholar who lived in the late 19th and early 20th century. Utilizing the legal system to encourage or discourage behavior is the theory underlying social engineering. A simple example of social engineering in law is the use of the tax code in the United States. If you own your own home you are allowed to deduct the interest on your home loan and the property taxes you pay in coming up with your taxable income. If you rent you are not allowed to deduct any of your rental payments in arriving at your taxable income. The government is clearly encouraging home ownership.

Frederich Karl von Savigny - Historical School of Jurisprudence

Savigny was a philosopher who believed that a nation's history and its laws go hand in hand. That is, if one looks at a nation's history and its common beliefs, the law is a reflection of that. For example, some of the Middle Eastern nations have laws that are based very closely to the dominant religion in that country. The history, culture and daily lives of many of the citizens involve their religious beliefs. That their laws would reflect their religious beliefs rings true under the historical school.

The Economic School of Jurisprudence

This philosophy has been discussed by many in the 20th and 21st centuries and certainly ties to the business model. In the economic theory it is believed that individuals work to maximize their own economic well-being. Consequently, societies pass laws that allow/encourage its citizenry to be successful and maximize its wealth. An example of this idea applied at the individual level is where a small business owner chooses not to sue a client over a broken contract even though she is legally in the right and will win the case. Long term, the client may bring more business and enrich the owner beyond the damages she has suffered in one transaction. Here, the business owner calculates the cost of litigation, the potential for short term and long term gain and ultimately makes an economic decision regarding the law.

Business and Social Responsibility

Businesses are faced with duties to myriad of parties. A community looks to a business for profit, goods and services and employment; but at what expense? For example, employment is a good thing for a community but the actions of a business can be detrimental as well. We have all read of successful companies that have polluted the environment. At times, businesses have had to shut down or move from a locality because of environmental concerns. Owners and employees look to business for their economic well being. But even these two parties can be at odds. That which is paid to the employee is that much less that is available to the business owner. Should a business contribute to the arts or charity in its own community? Some contend that businesses should give to charity, as it is part of the responsibility a business has in its community. Others, (Milton Friedman, the noted economist, is the best known) believe that business has the duty to gain the most profit possible and enrich the shareholders without being distracted by charity and similar concerns. The argument is that the shareholders can and should choose individually what to do with those profits.

While profit maximization is an important duty any business has, it is a mistake to take the short-term view and maximize profits while disregarding the bigger picture in society. When that happens the law steps in and limits the things business can do. That is, if business does not regulate itself, the government will eventually step in. For example, early in the industrial revolution in the late 19th century some of the successful industrialists used their profits to buy up the competition, or price cut their products to put their competitors out of business and create a monopoly for themselves. In 1890 the federal government passed the *Sherman Antitrust Act* which limited businesses ability to reduce competition and monopolize an industry. The government went farther in 1914 in passing the *Clayton Act*, which strengthened the *Sherman Act*. The Clayton Act restricted unfair practices such as tying contracts and interlocking boards of directors, which substantially lessened competition in certain industries.

In the chapters covering the law of agency later in the course we will look at statutes that protect employees from certain behaviors by businesses. Time and again we see the government will step in when businesses do not regulate themselves.

Guidance in Business Ethics

As individuals there are many guides that can help us with ethical decisions. Some individuals choose to use their religion as a basis for deciding what is right and wrong. Others find that a set of rules or a specific rule like the golden rule ("do unto others as you would have them do unto you") can be the basis for ethical decision making. Lawrence Kohlberg, a noted psychologist, believed that individuals progress through moral stages in life. In the first level one is motivated by the fear of punishment and the expectation of reward, much the way a young child sees the world. Kohlberg called this level the preconventional level. In the second level one is motivated to meet the expectations of groups such as family, friends etc. seeking love, trust and acceptance. Kohlberg called the second level the conventional stage of moral development. The third stage, called the post conventional stage of moral development, is that where one is motivated to do what is right for the correct underlying moral principles. Here one is not concerned with how others may think of him, rather, he wants to do what is morally and ethically correct. Kohlberg believed that most adults operate at the preconventional and conventional stage.

In any event, we as individuals can decide upon our ethics in any of several ways. Our upbringing, environment, life experiences and perhaps our stage of moral development come to play in ethical decisions. Ethical behavior and ethical decisions can be more difficult for businesses in that a business is made up of several individuals whose morals may be quite different. Should a business engage in advertising that is effective but some see as deceptive in a highly competitive marketplace? Does being competitive include spreading information to potential customers that a competitor's product is under investigation for safety violations and the like?

One philosopher's approach that comes up with regularity in the business arena is Immanuel Kant (1724-1804). His *categorical imperative* theorizes that individuals (and therefore individual businesses) must evaluate the consequences of their decisions as though everyone in society acted the same way. For example, imagine that as an employee you have the opportunity to embezzle $10 per week from your employer without being caught. That amounts to a $520 'raise' over the year. What are the logical consequences if all 1000 employees in the firm did the same over a year? A $520 loss to the business becomes over a half a million-dollar loss.

Some pundits contend that the term 'business ethics' is an oxymoron like 'military intelligence' or 'peacekeeping missile'. Do you agree with the pundits?

Chapter 3

Classifications of Law

Ignorantia juris non excusat. (Ignorance of the law is no excuse) - Legal Maxim

One of the first things that makes understanding the law somewhat manageable is learning how the law is classified or broken down. Like many complex subjects, if the law is broken down into its simpler parts, comprehension is easier.

Earlier we defined law simply as the set of rules that tells us what we can and cannot do. In fact there is more to the law than that. For example there are things we must do - like pay taxes, things we can do - like drive a car, and things we cannot do - like steal a car. So in law we have duties - things we must do, and we have rights - things we can do. Generally, if one has a right to something, someone has a duty to deliver it. If I have paid you $200,000 for your house, I have a right to receive it and you have a duty to deliver it. A right is the legal capacity to require another to deliver something, perform or refrain from performing an act. A duty is a legal obligation that requiring an individual to perform or refrain from performing an act.

American law is broken down first into substantive and procedural law. Substantive law is the law that creates or sets the rights and duties of individuals or groups. Procedural law establishes the rules by which we enforce substantive law. For example, traffic laws are substantive laws. Say you get a traffic ticket. You allegedly were caught going 40 miles per hour in a 25 miles per hour zone. You are certain that the police officer made a mistake. You take the ticket, drive to the nearest court house and find a court that is open wait for a break and say, "Yoo-hoo, Your Honor, I need you to hear my case right now!" It turns out that you have wandered into family court where the judge is hearing a child custody case. Would the judge, could the judge hear your case? Of course not. You have proceeded incorrectly. There is a procedure you must follow to fight the ticket. This falls under procedural law. You have probably heard of due process under the law as a constitutional right. This is the part of law that ensures that both sides follow the same set of rules in dealing with substantive law.

Another classification of law is that of public law and private law. Public law is the law that deals with our relationship with the government. Criminal law and constitutional law fall here. Private law deals with our relationship with one another. Civil law falls here.

Criminal law, part of public law, is the law that determines duties that we owe the entire community. Civil law, part of private law, deals with the duties we owe one another. For example, imagine that tomorrow morning you get up in the morning, go outside to pick up your newspaper and your neighbor is outside and tells you that someone broke into her home and ransacked her house. One of your first thoughts is that you hope they catch the criminal because this individual is clearly a threat to the community as a whole. This act falls under criminal law. When the thief is caught, the government, representing the public will try him or her.

You go back into your house after talking to your neighbor, open the newspaper and find that IBM is suing Intel over some trade secrets that employees have allegedly stole. You don't own stock in either company so you are probably not particularly interested in the lawsuit. After all, the civil lawsuit is a private matter between the two companies.

The following is a brief summary of law classification and some key terms that are important to know:

Substantive Law

Creates and defines legal rights and responsibilities. Business law such as contract and agency law fall here.

Procedural Law

Rules by which substantive law is enforced. In a criminal lawsuit the government must follow criminal procedure in trying an individual. In a civil lawsuit each party must follow civil procedure throughout the suit ensuring both parties follow the same set of rules.

Public Law

Powers of the government and how it is applied to individuals. Criminal, constitutional and administrative law are part of public law.

Private Law

Law that governs relationships between individuals and individual entities. Contract law, the law of sales, agency law, corporations, partnerships and property law fall under private law. Plaintiff

Plaintiff

Individual or individual entity who files a lawsuit. If you decide to sue a vendor for not delivering goods that were promised to you, you are the plaintiff.

Defendant

Individual or individual entity that is sued. The defendant defends against the legal action. In the above action, if you are the individual being sued for non-delivery of those goods, you are the defendant.

Civil Action

A lawsuit initiated against a private party or parties. If you sue a customer for non-payment of a bill, you will institute a civil action.

Criminal Action

A lawsuit initiated by the government against and individual or individual entity for the breaking of a criminal law. If you rob a convenience store and are caught, the government will institute a criminal action against you.

Criminal and Civil Suits

You can be liable both criminally and civilly in a worst-case scenario. For example, if you drive drunk and get in an accident, the government will initiate a criminal suit or action against you for driving under the influence; and the party who you injured in the accident may sue you in civil court for damages she incurred as a result of your behavior.

Differences between Civil and Criminal Law

There are some dramatic differences between civil and criminal law that should be noted. In civil law an individual initiates the lawsuit. In criminal law the government (the federal, state or local government) initiates the suit. To prevail in a civil lawsuit you must prove your case by a preponderance (a majority) of the evidence. In a criminal suit you must prove your case beyond a reasonable doubt - a much higher burden of proof than in a civil suit. The remedies available in a civil lawsuit are monetary damages or equitable remedies. Remedies at equity include specific performance - requiring someone to do something (like deliver goods that are under contract), injunction - requiring someone to stop doing something (like picketing in front of your building), reformation - having the court rewrite an agreement due to some mutual mistake by parties in a contract, or rescission - where the court invalidates a contract. In a criminal lawsuit the remedies include the death penalty, prison and jail time, fines and probation.

The Order of Precedence in Law

One question that comes up regularly is which law takes precedence over another? There is a relatively clear hierarchy of law with the United States Constitution at the highest level. All laws must conform to the basis of law in the U.S. Constitution. From there the order of precedence is as follows:

Treaties and Federal Statutes

Treaties are agreements between nations and federal statutes are legislative laws made by congress and the president. Federal statutes also include executive orders issued by the president. Statutes enacted by the legislative branch of the government are often referred to as codified law because they are written into law or code books organized by topic.

Federal Administrative Law

Rules and regulations made by administrative agencies like the Environmental Protection Agency (EPA). Administrative Agencies are agencies created by the government to regulate certain areas of our society. These include taxation (the IRS and the Treasury Department), transportation, public health and so forth.

Federal Common Law

Decisions made by federal court that do not conflict with federal statutes.

State Constitutions

Ultimate law at the state level that establishes the power and limitations of the state government.

State Statutes

Legislative laws and executive orders at the state level.

State Administrative Law

Rules and regulations made at the state level by state agencies like the Department of Consumer Affairs.

State Common Law

Decisions made by state courts that do not conflict with higher laws

Local Ordinances

Statutes made by local bodies at the county and city level. Examples of these include traffic laws, building codes and similar laws.

Chapter 4

Jurisdiction, Courts, Civil Procedure

"Lawsuits consume time, and money, and rest, and friends" - George Herbert

We have looked at the history of law, some philosophy of law and how law is classified. Now to the practical. How does one file a civil suit? Where will the case wind up and why?

As to the filing of a civil suit, we will walk through each procedural step and examine how a lawsuit progresses. How about where the case is heard? Is it in state court, federal court, trial court, appeals court? The answer is, it depends on the circumstances of the case.

Jurisdiction is the power and authority of a court to hear and decide a given case. To lawfully assume jurisdiction, a court must have subject matter jurisdiction, and jurisdiction over the parties.

Subject matter jurisdiction is the authority of a court to hear and decide a given case. There are three types of jurisdiction:

Exclusive Federal Subject Matter Jurisdiction

These are cases that will be heard exclusively in a federal court. These issues include copyright, patent, bankruptcy, federal crimes, antitrust, suits against the United States and specific federal statutes. These cases cannot be heard in state court. For example, should you go through bankruptcy or if your company is involved in an antitrust matter (as Microsoft recently has) the hearing will be only at the federal court level.

Concurrent Federal Jurisdiction

These are cases that are shared with the states. These cases can be heard in either federal or state court. There are two types of concurrent federal jurisdiction, federal question jurisdiction and diversity jurisdiction. Federal question jurisdiction is any case that arises under the constitution, statutes or treaties of the United States. There is no dollar amount tied to a federal question issue.

Diversity jurisdiction takes place when there is a diversity of citizenship between the plaintiffs and defendants (meaning the plaintiff and defendant are from different states) and the amount of the controversy exceeds $75,000. If both conditions exist, then the case can be heard in either federal or state court.

Exclusive State Jurisdiction

All other matters not described above fall under exclusive state jurisdiction. A federal court (including the U.S. Supreme Court) has no power to hear a case under exclusive state jurisdiction. With respect to those matters, states have exclusive jurisdiction.

Jurisdiction Over the Parties

This is the power of the court to bind specific parties to a lawsuit. There are three ways that a party can be brought to court:

In personam jurisdiction

In rem jurisdiction

Attachment jurisdiction

In personam jursidiction is having the power to bind the parties to a lawsuit based on claims against a specific person or persons. A court successfully obtains jurisdiction over a party by service of process (the delivery of a summons) within the state which the court is located or outside the jurisdiction of the court where the party has sufficient "minimum contacts" with the jurisdiction to allow for the "long arm statutes" to apply.

An example of in personam jurisdiction is where you might sue a customer who owes you money and has chosen not to pay. The customer lives in your county in California and so to begin the lawsuit you will have a summons delivered to her. She falls under the jurisdiction of the state court.

If your customer lived outside California (your state), but entered into a contract in the state, owned property there, committed a tort in California, or transacted business in California and that business is the subject matter of a lawsuit; then your customer, the defendant, has enough minimum contacts for the long-arm statutes to apply. These laws allow the court to obtain jurisdiction over defendants who do not reside in the state. The long-arm statutes can be utilized provided that the exercise of the jurisdiction is consistent with traditional notions of fair play and justice.

In rem jurisdiction allow courts in a state to exercise jurisdiction over property, despite a lack of citizenship in the state. For example, you might reside in Arizona and own a commercial building that you rent in California. The renter is an individual from Oregon. If the basis of the dispute were the rental unit, the appropriate trial court would have in rem jurisdiction to hear the case in California.

Attachment jurisdiction (also called quasi in rem) allows a court jurisdiction over property that is not specifically part of a lawsuit. For example, assume you are a resident of California and obtain a judgment against a citizen of Oregon. The Oregon citizen has a bank account in California. Attachment jurisdiction allows you to seize or attach the bank account in order to satisfy your court judgment against the Oregonian.

Venue

Venue is a term that should not be confused with jurisdiction. Venue deals with the appropriate geographical location of a trial. A court trying a case follows the policy that the case should be heard in the geographical location where the issue causing the lawsuit occurred, or where the opposing parties reside. On occasion, there may be so much pretrial publicity that seating a group of impartial jurors appears impossible. Consequently, one of the parties will move for a change of venue. If the court agrees that a fair trial is impossible in a given area, then the location of the trial will be changed.

Court Systems

We have determined that jurisdiction is the basis for which court and where a lawsuit is heard. The next issue is to determine the structure of the state and federal courts. Each state has its own court system and there is a separate system of federal courts.

Trial courts are the courts where issues of fact and law are heard. They are what we usually think of when a trial takes place. In the federal court system the U.S. District Courts are the trial courts that have original, general jurisdiction to hear cases involving federal matters. There are also specialized courts at the federal level that hear cases of a particular type. These courts include bankruptcy, tax, federal claims, the patent and trademark office and others.

At the state level in California there are also trial courts of general and specialized jurisdiction. The courts that are specialized are called inferior courts and are courts like traffic court and family court. The trial courts are municipal and superior courts where non-specialized matters are heard.

Both the state and federal systems have courts of appeals. These courts hear cases that have been appealed from the trial level courts where they examine the record and determine if the trial court committed an error. If the error is such that it affected the appellant's rights or duties the appellate court can do the following:

> Remand the case - send it back to trial again
> Reverse the judgment - set aside the trial judgment
> Modify the judgment - change the trial courts ruling

Or the court of appeals can affirm the decision of the trial court if it is found that there was no prejudicial error. The appeals courts focus on issues of law, and generally they do not focus on issues of fact. So the courts consider whether the law was applied correctly and do not hear new evidence. The appeals courts review transcripts of the trial, consider briefs filed by attorneys and listen to oral arguments by the attorneys. Appeals courts do not consider evidence or testimony.

The highest court in the land is the U.S. Supreme Court. The principal function of the Supreme Court is to review decisions by the Federal Courts of Appeals and the state supreme courts. It is an appellate court.

Each state has its own Supreme Court, which functions as the highest appellate court in that state. It is an appellate court that has the final say in all issues of law in the state except for the federal issues that can ultimately be decided by the U.S. Supreme Court.

Civil Procedure

One area of the law that businessmen and businesswomen should be familiar with is the chronology of a civil lawsuit. When a business issue winds up in court, it is most often heard in civil court. Understanding the steps in a private lawsuit allows you to make better decisions in whether or not to sue, choosing an attorney and recognizing risk in a business transaction.

Step One - The Alleged Wrong

It is inevitable in business that things will go wrong from time to time. Businesses will not deliver goods on time, something delivered will be defective, someone does not pay, or a customer is injured on your premises. Any of those issues will cause a problem. How is it solved?

If you answered "Sue the bums!" you probably won't be in business very long. Good businesses work their problems out at a low level and take a long-term view. Most important, businesses consider the issue of risk versus return. There are plenty of times that we can be legally right and win a case in court and lose a customer or a valued vendor after winning the case. The last thing a business wants to do is win a pyrrhic victory, where a battle is won and the war is lost. Consequently, successful businesses try to resolve the issue informally. Effective businesses have individuals who are skilled at conflict resolution and they always try to look at the big picture when problems arise.

Step Two - Alternative Dispute Resolution

Suing someone is expensive, time consuming and risky. When an informal resolution cannot be reached there are conflict resolution methods other than a lawsuit that are available to individuals and businesses.

Conciliation

In this process a third party acts as a mediator or conciliator between the two parties involved in the dispute. For example, it is fairly common for union contracts to have a clause that requires conciliation between a manager and an employee when there is a potential contractual dispute. For example, say you have a vendor (XYZ) who is supposed to deliver a computer system to your business by December 1 of the current year. In the contract it states that the computer system should be able to access certain web sites within two minutes and handle up to 100 e-mails per minute. The contract is worth $95,000.

The company delivers the system on December 15, 14 days late, partly because your purchasing manager gave the wrong shipping address. The firm delivering the system incurs extra shipping charges, but does not charge your firm. One of the XYZ sales people admit privately that the system probably would not have been delivered to you until December 10, because of some manufacturing problems.

The system does not work as perfectly as expected. Accessing some of the web sites takes longer than the two minutes and it appears that the system handles only about 60 e-mails per minute instead of the 100 promised. Your company decides that it is unhappy with XYZ's performance and is considering not paying XYZ and suing them for damages. There is a problem though, in that your company needs the system and is using it now. Moreover, some in your company say that some of the system problems are not XYZ's fault, but the fault of the web sites you need to contact. Your company was supposed to have paid $40,000 to XYZ one month before delivery, but only paid $20,000 because it was short of cash. The remaining $75,000 is now due and payable (with $20,000 being a month late). XYZ is demanding payment, and is considering suing your company if you don't pay soon.

Clearly, the problem is somewhat complex, with no clear winner or loser in this contract. This is typically the case in business disputes. There is no evil villain, rather each party has its own problems to defend against and needs to work things out.

If both companies cannot reach an informal solution, then conciliation might be tried. Both companies would agree on a conciliator, a neutral third party, who would work with both parties to try and reach a solution. The conciliator will try to open lines of communication, get both parties talking with one another or serve as an intermediary if both parties do not want to meet with one another. Often, the conciliator is an individual who has a relationship with both parties. It might be an attorney that has advised both companies on matters in the past, or a former salesperson that worked for both companies. The focus of the conciliator is to get the two parties to reach an agreement. The conciliator does not make a decision as to how the issue should be decided.

Mediation

Another form of dispute resolution is mediation, which might be tried in this case. Here, the mediator is a neutral third party chosen by the two parties who does all the things a conciliator does, but offers solutions to the issue. These solutions are non-binding, but often can effect a settlement between the parties.

Arbitration

In arbitration, the parties choose a neutral third party to hear and decide the dispute. The arbitrator hears arguments and reviews evidence and issues a binding decision called an award. There are some clear advantages of arbitration over litigation. First, often an arbitrator has special expertise in area of dispute, allowing for a higher quality resolution than may be possible in court. Second, the process is informal and tends to cost less and take less time. Third, arbitration is conducted in private, unlike a trial, which is a matter of public record. Consequently, there tends to be little or no issue of unwanted publicity for the parties involved.

Some contracts call for alternative dispute resolution as part of terms of the agreement. This helps ensure that a dispute can be resolved at a relatively low, less expensive level than the courts. It is common for many union employment contracts to have a process for dispute resolution between union employees and managers that requires conciliation, then mediation, and if those don't work, then arbitration. If the example of your company and XYZ had an arbitration clause, then the two companies would probably stay out of court in resolving the dispute.

There is a possibility of judicial review of an arbitration award. The awards must follow law and the arbitration hearing must have followed due process. Additionally, the courts can overrule an arbitrator's award if the arbitrator exceeded his authority; there is evidence of fraud or other types of misconduct.

It should be noted that it is fairly common to have an arbitration clause in many international business contracts. The risk of doing business overseas is compounded when a company thinks of having to hire experts to navigate a customer or vendor's legal system because of a lawsuit. Consequently, companies will often put in an arbitration clause picking a neutral third country for the arbitration. For example, companies from Greece and the United States might pick Paris, France as the location for the arbitration. Then, the contract might call for an arbitration tribunal made up of a panel of three arbitrators - one chosen by the U.S. Company, one chosen by the Greek Company, and a third arbitrator agreed upon by both companies. In the event that arbitration is required, the contract calls out for the process of the hearing.

Step Three - Litigation - Retain an Attorney

Assuming that informal resolution of the dispute fails, then the next step will be a lawsuit. The first step in a lawsuit is to retain an attorney. A company may have a law firm on retainer already or it may need to find a lawyer. In any event, the attorney will get the process going for the firm.

Step Four - Complaint and Summons

The attorney representing the plaintiff will file the complaint with the appropriate court. The complaint states the plaintiff's claims in separate, numbered paragraphs. It names the parties to the lawsuit, alleges the facts, and indicates the law that was violated, and contains the legal relief or remedy requested by the plaintiff.

So in our example of your company and XYZ, the complaint would name both parties to the suit, indicate the alleged contract breach and request monetary damages.

The complaint will generate a summons, which notifies the defendant that he or she is being sued. The summons is served to the defendant by a process server, a sheriff or another government official. In most cases the summons is delivered in person along with the complaint so the defendant received proper notice (is given due process) of the lawsuit. In some cases the summons may be delivered by registered mail for out of state defendants depending on the long arm statutes.

Step Five - The Answer

At this point, the defendant has been notified that he or she is being sued and has a certain amount of time (usually around 30 days) to respond to the complaint. If the defendant does not respond to the complaint, a default judgment will be entered against him or her. So in our example of XYZ and your company, if XYZ fails to respond in any way, a default judgment will be entered against XYZ.

The other possibility that XYZ has instead of responding with an answer is to make a pretrial motion contesting that the court where the complaint has been issued does not have jurisdiction over it or that the suit is barred by the statute of limitations. XYZ might move that the suit be dismissed for failure to state a claim. This is called a demurrer. With a demurrer XYZ would allege that even if everything in the complaint were true, that your company has no right to the remedy requested.

In most cases however, the defendant responds by filing an answer. The answer may contain any and all of the following:

> Admissions - the defendant admits to something in the complaint

> Denials - the defendant denies something in the complaint

> Affirmative defenses - the defendant admits to something in the complaint, but claims the defendant is not liable because the plaintiff was negligent or something of the like

> Counterclaim - the defendant requests a judgment from the plaintiff for damages the plaintiff caused the defendant

If the defendant presents a counterclaim the plaintiff will have to respond with a reply which can contain admissions, denials and affirmative defenses.

The complaint and the answer taken together are called the pleadings portion of the suit.

At this point, there might not be any issues of fact to dispute. In rare cases, the complaint and answer agree on all of the factual issues. When that happens, one of the parties may move for a judgment on the pleadings. The judge would make a final, binding decision that would be based on the merits of the case presented in the pleadings.

Step Six - Discovery

The next step in the civil suit is the pretrial discovery process. This is where information is exchanged by the opposing parties in the lawsuit. Both parties engage in several activities designed to discover facts of the case about the other party and its witnesses.

Discovery is the right of a party to a lawsuit to obtain information about "any matter, not privileged, that is relevant to the subject matter involved in the pending action...if the matter either is itself admissible in evidence or appears reasonably calculated to lead to the discovery of admissible evidence." (California Code of Civil Procedure Section 2017)

Some of the tools of discovery are:

Depositions - The oral examination of witness under oath. The witness' testimony is preserved in writing and under some circumstances is admissible at trial.

Interrogatories - A written question asked by one party to another party, who must answer under oath and in writing. Answers to interrogatories are usually answered by, or with the assistance of counsel.

Demands for - A party can demand the right to inspect and copy documents and other physical
Production evidence in the possession of an opposing party.
of Documents
and Objects

Requests for - Procedure by which one party forces the other party to admit or deny the truth
Admissions of a relevant fact. For example, you might be asked to admit that you own a certain car and were driving it on a given day when an accident occurred.

Physical and - Examination by a physician of the opposing party to determine extent of injuries
Mental
Examinations

The discovery phase of the trial enables both parties to get a relatively clear view of the strength of each side's case. Often, during discovery, an out of court settlement can be reached because one or both parties become more fully aware of the nature and possible outcome of the dispute.

Summary Judgment

On occasion, the discovery phase will generate such clear evidence that there are no issues of fact that need be disputed. There is no need for a trial because it is just a question of how the law should be applied. In this case, one of the parties will move for a summary judgment. The motion is supported by the evidence presented in discovery. If in fact, there are no factual issues that need to be heard by a jury, then a judge will grant the motion and rule for one of the parties.

Step Seven - Pretrial Conference

The pretrial conference is a conference between the judge and the opposing attorneys where one of the main objectives is to settle the case before going to trial. Additionally, the focus of the conference is to simplify the issues at trial should the case go forward.

Step Eight - Trial

The next step in civil procedure is the trial. This is where the issues of fact will be heard by the jury and the issues of law will be considered by the judge. The trial is broken down into several steps.

Jury Selection

Jury selection is referred to as *voir dire*, which is the preliminary examination of potential jurors. In examining potential jurors, the parties have an unlimited number of challenges for cause, which allow a party to prevent a juror from serving if the juror appears biased. Additionally, the parties also have a limited number of peremptory challenges, which allow for the disqualification of a juror for no cause whatsoever.

Opening Statements

Once the jury has been seated each attorney makes an opening statement which summarizes what each expects to prove in the trial.

Plaintiff's Case

The plaintiff begins with direct examination of witnesses called by the plaintiff. Each witness is subject to cross-examination by the defendant's attorney.

On occasion one of the parties will move for a directed verdict at this point in the trial. The contention is that based on what has gone forward thus far, there are no issues of fact to be resolved and that one party (the moving party) should prevail. In many cases like these, the defense moves for a directed verdict, contending that the plaintiff failed to prove his or her case. If the judge concurs, then the trial ends and the motion made by the defense is granted.

Defendant's Case

The defendant then begins to make his or her case through direct examination of witnesses. The focus of the defense is to rebut the plaintiff's case and to prove any cross complaints the defense may have alleged against the plaintiff. The plaintiff has the right to cross-examine each of the defense witnesses.

Once the defense has completed calling witnesses, the plaintiff has the right to call witnesses and rebut the defendant's case. This is called a rebuttal. The defendant's attorney can do the same in a process called the rejoinder.

Closing Arguments

Once the presentation of evidence from both sides has been completed, the attorneys present their closing arguments urging the jury to find for their respective clients.

Jury Instructions, Verdict

At that point the judge issues jury instructions. This is where the judge explains to the jury how the law is applied in the particular case before them.

The jury deliberates and reaches a verdict in favor of the plaintiff or defendant.

Motions after the Trial

If the losing party believes that the jury has made an error in judgment and the decision made by the jury is not supported in law, he or she will move for a *judgment n.o.v.* (judgment notwithstanding the verdict). If the judge agrees, then the judge will find for the losing party and set the jury verdict aside. If the judge disagrees, then the judge will deny the motion and enter the verdict for the prevailing party.

The losing party can also make a motion for a new trial. The judge may grant this if he or she believes that the jury made an error in judgment, but not so much as to grant the losing party a *judgment n.o.v.*

The case may be appealed if it is determined that there was an error of law made by the trial court that is considered prejudicial. The losing party may file an appeal and will appeal on the basis of law. As discussed earlier, the court of appeals does not hear evidence. It reviews the transcripts, attorney's briefs, and sometimes hears oral arguments from the attorneys to decide if there was an error of law.

If the case is not appealed, or if the appeals court affirms the judgment (assuming the losing party appealed) then the losing party is expected to pay the judgment. If he or she does not pay the judgment, the prevailing party will request a writ of execution from the clerk of the court demanding payment. This will allow the sheriff to present the writ demanding payment. If the payment is not forthcoming a process can begin which allows for the sale of property and/or garnishment against the losing party's employer.

Chronology of a Lawsuit

Alleged wrong - informal resolution fails

Retain attorney

Plaintiff files complaint - summons is generated

Defendant responds or files answer

Judgment on the Pleadings

Pretrial Discovery
    depositions
    interrogatories
    requests for admissions
    inspection demands
    physical and mental examinations
    expert witness disclosure

Summary Judgment

Trial date set
Pre-trial conference
Trial
    motions
    jury selection - voir dire
        peremptory challenges
        challenges for cause

    opening statements
    plaintiff's case

        direct examination of witnesses called by plaintiff
        cross examination by defense of witnesses called by plaintiff

Directed Verdict

    defendant's case

        direct examination of witnesses called by defendant
        cross examination by plaintiff of witnesses called by defendant
    closing arguments
    jury instructions
    deliberation
    verdict

    motions - judgment notwithstanding the verdict

    entry of judgment

    appeal

Chapter 5

Constitutional and Administrative Law

"What's the constitution between friends?" - *Timothy John Campbell, U.S. Congressman, remark to President Grover Cleveland Alexander*

As we have discussed before, the U.S. Constitution is the supreme law of the land. It defines the rights and responsibilities that citizens have in our country and defines the relationship between the state and federal government. Perhaps most important, it limits the power of the government in its relationship with individuals.

From a business perspective there are some key concepts to be aware of from the constitution. You might remember that earlier it was mentioned that there is an order of precedence in law that begins with the federal constitution, then moves to federal statutes and so forth. There are certain basic principles that the constitution spells out. Those fundamental principles, powers and limitations on the government are summarized below:

Separation of Powers

The constitution grants separate, distinct powers among the legislative branch (congress), the executive branch (president) and the judiciary (Supreme Court and the federal judiciary). These three branches fall under a system of checks and balances designed to keep one branch from having more power or greater influence than another.

Federalism

Federalism is the structure of the division of power between the federal and state governments. As a general rule, while many rights to govern are held by the states; the federal power to govern and regulate has been broadly interpreted over the years. Consequently, over the years congress has been given the latitude to regulate interstate and foreign commerce to a very high degree. This gives the federal government extraordinary power in business and commerce in the United States under the concept of federalism.

Federal Supremacy

As mentioned earlier, the U.S. Constitution is the supreme law of the land and when there is a conflict between a federal and state law, the federal law preempts the state law taking precedence over it. This falls under the concept of federal supremacy.

Judicial Review

Under this doctrine, the judiciary is able to keep the legislative and executive branch from enacting laws that are contrary to the constitution. The courts, (with the supreme court having the final say) are empowered to review laws that have been passed by congress, acts of the executive branch and lower court rulings to ensure that the governmental actions do not violate the constitution. If those laws or acts conflict with the constitution, the courts will invalidate the action.

Federal Commerce Power

Federal commerce power has been interpreted by the Supreme Court in a broad sense, which has had the effect of allowing the federal government to regulate the economy while limiting state regulations that inhibit interstate commerce. Consequently, between congress and federal administrative agencies, the bulk of regulations and laws that businesses follow come from the federal government.

Federal Fiscal Power

As we are all aware, the federal government has the power to tax and spend. In addition, the federal government has the power to borrow and coin money as well as the power of eminent domain.

The federal government's power to tax is relatively obvious to anyone who has filled out a tax form. As we look at the cost of our defense, regulation and the like, the power of the government to spend money is obvious as well. Hearing about our federal deficit makes the power to borrow money easy to comprehend, and the government's power to coin money is understandable by the youngest of school children.

The power of eminent domain is one that should be briefly examined. This is the power that government has that allows it to take private property. There are two things that must happen when the power of eminent domain is exercised. First, the property taken must be used for the public. Second, just compensation must be paid to the citizen who gives up his or her property. If the public benefits in an eminent domain case (for example putting a freeway through a city) and fair market value is offered and paid to the owners of the condemned property, then the eminent domain action will hold.

States also share many of these fiscal powers. As we all know, states have income, sales and related taxes that seem to burden us all. We can see how states spend money on schools and regulation. Moreover, states borrow money through bonds and similar debt instruments.

Government Powers and Limitations

While we see a great deal of power held by the government in the areas of commerce and fiscal issues, the federal and state governments are limited in what it can do in these areas as well. Certain limitations on government apply specifically to business. One example of government limitations of power is in the contract clause of the constitution. There is a prohibition from states modifying contracts retroactively after they have been made.

Another area of government limitation of power is the first amendment of the constitution, which guarantees the right of free speech. This in essence allows citizens to criticize and question our government and its officials without fear of imprisonment or other sanctions. Commercial speech, exercised by firms, is protected but to a lesser degree. One of the issues that commercial speech must deal with is whether or not advertisements and the like concern lawful activities and are not misleading.

Free speech is not absolutely free in our society. We cannot exercise free speech rights to the degree that another individual is defamed by what we say. This means we have no right to injure another's reputation in a false manner. Moreover, certain types of speech are not protected. For example, threatening speech and pornographic speech are not protected by the first amendment.

Most of us are aware that we are not allowed to yell 'fire' in a crowded movie house because it is unsafe. First amendment protection only goes so far.

The constitution also limits the government's power in requiring due process of the law before depriving anyone of life, liberty or property. Additionally, equal protection under the law is guaranteed in the constitution meaning that similarly situated persons must be treated similarly by the government.

Limiting government power in the constitution has been instrumental in creating and maintaining the strongest economic environment for business in the world over the past two hundred years. Business has flourished in the United States partially because the government is less of a burden to business than it is in other countries.

Administrative Law

That is not to say however, that there is minimal regulation of business in the United States. Administrative agencies regulate business to such a high degree that some refer to administrative agencies as the "fourth branch" of government in our country. Administrative agencies exist at all levels of government - federal, state and local.

Administrative agencies got their start in the late nineteenth century when congress realized that certain parts of the economy were so specialized that the details of lawmaking to regulate businesses were more than they could do effectively. Consequently, the government delegated power to administrative agencies enabling them to make rules and regulations that have the same force and effect as law. Think of the Environmental Protection Agency, the Food and Drug Administration and the Securities Exchange Commission at the federal level and of the Department of Real Estate at the state level as classic examples of administrative agencies that regulate parts of our society.

An administrative agency is empowered to make rules and interpret law the following ways:

Substantive Rulemaking	Making and issuing rules based on an agency's delegated power referred to as legislative rules
Interpretive Rulemaking	Interpreting rules based on existing statutes
Statement of Policy	Explaining how an agency plans to proceed in implementing or enforcing certain rules and regulations

Administrative agencies are also given the power to enforce the law in the areas where administrative law is violated. Agencies have the right to investigate conduct when it is suspected that an individual, group or company has violated the law.

Once an investigation is completed, the agency has the power to adjudicate the issue. Agencies have broad power to settle these disputes and can do so informally or formally. They can (and are encouraged by congress) to use negotiation, mediation and arbitration in settling disputes. Moreover, administrative agencies will advise parties who are thought to be in violation of regulatory rules how to comply with the regulations.

One of the concerns involving administrative agencies is that it is possible that some may overstep their bounds. What can a citizen or business do if an administrative agency acts improperly? There are some safeguards in place in that an agency has with public disclosure requirements so the public and other parts of government are notified of agency actions. The Freedom of Information Act allows the public access to records of administrative agencies. The Government in Sunshine Act requires public meetings of many of the administrative agencies at the federal level. These two acts help ensure that the public has the opportunity to be informed of agency policy and actions. Freedom of speech and freedom of the press allow for publication and comment on acts of administrative agencies (and of the government as a whole) thus helping ensure that the agencies are accountable to the public. Additionally, both the executive and legislative branches of government have oversight and budget control of the agencies. Judicial review of an agency's actions is available to challenge an agency's actions if it oversteps its bounds as well.

An agency can find itself being reviewed by the judiciary if it:

Exceeds its authority

Improperly interprets applicable law

Acts contrary to the procedural requirements of law

Violates the constitution in any actions

Acts arbitrarily or capriciously

Reaches a conclusion not supported by substantial evidence

So while administrative agencies have a great deal of power to regulate business in our economy, so too are they subject to the scrutiny of review as well.

Chapter 6

Torts

"Fools and obstinate men make lawyers rich" – Barber, <u>*The Book of 1000 Proverbs*</u>

Overview

Tort law is part of private, civil law. Each of us has civil liability in the eyes of the law for our actions when it affects others. Often, when we think of wrongdoing we think of a criminal act. We are indeed criminally liable for our actions if we meet the requisites for a crime, but we also carry civil liability as well.

For example, say that you get angry with a colleague and hit him in the arm with a tire iron. His arm is broken by your act. A police officer witnesses the altercation and arrests you. You wind up being tried in criminal court for assault and battery and are sentenced to six months in county jail. The jail time is the criminal liability that you face. Your colleague incurs $25,000 in medical bills and has to be off his job for several months while he recuperates. The total cost of the injury and lost time come to $60,000. Whom does he look to for damages? The answer is you. You caused his injury and you now have personal liability for the damages caused by your behavior. You might think that you cannot be sued since you've been to court once and were convicted. "Isn't there a constitutional guarantee against double jeopardy?" you might ask. There is a constitutional right against criminal double jeopardy, but you can certainly be liable both criminally and civilly for the same act. So after you get out of jail, have probably lost your job, your spouse has left you and your friends no longer call; you get to defend yourself against a $60,000 lawsuit that you will most likely lose. Next time, keep your temper in check. You'll stay out of jail and you'll keep your money.

Tort liability falls under the following areas:

Intentional - liability for an intentional act. For example, you stab a colleague because you're in a bad mood.

Reckless - liability for an act that is grossly careless with a disregard for potential high risk of harm. For example, you swing a baseball bat in a crowded area, not intending to hurt anyone, but not taking care to avoid hitting others as well. You hit a bystander who is injured by your act.

Negligent - "conduct that falls below the standard established by law for the protection of others against an unreasonable risk of harm," (Restatement). For example, you don't drive as carefully as you should and accidentally hit a pedestrian in a crosswalk. You did not intend to hit the pedestrian, and you were not reckless. Still you were not as careful as you should have been.

Strict Liability - liability without fault. In certain activities, you can be liable for injuries sustained by another despite the fact that you were not reckless or negligent. For example, if you are engaging in abnormally dangerous activities like using dynamite to demolish a building, and someone is injured you may be liable for those injuries.

Intentional Torts

Intentional torts do not require an evil or hostile intent, they require that the actor desires the consequences of his act. Intentional torts are divided between torts against persons and torts against property. Common intentional torts against persons are discussed below.

Battery *?*

Battery is the unlawful touching of another. We all have a right to expect that we can move about in society without being punched, pulled, hit, shot or stabbed. A battery can take place when someone hits you in the face, knocks a hat off your head or rips a purse out of your hand. While we do not have to be physically touched, part of our person (our clothing, something we are holding onto) must be touched.

Battery does not protect us from reasonable touching. For example, if someone accidentally runs into you at a crowded football game, or touches your shoulder to get your attention, a battery has not been committed.

Assault

Assault is what some call the "heartbeat tort". Assault occurs when we are put in immediate fear of being battered. For example, someone holds a gun to your face or rushes toward you in a manner that would cause any reasonable person to fear he or she was about to be hit.

Assault requires immediacy. If I threaten to stab you next week sometime, assault has not been committed.

Hopefully, most business people will not have to worry about assault and battery. However, there have been cases at bars and cocktail lounges where bouncers and security employees have assaulted or battered customers creating liability for themselves and the business owners.

False Imprisonment — *have to be aware that you do not have save exist*

False imprisonment is the intentional confinement of another without justification or permission of the individual being detained. It can be for a very short time and as long as there is no safe or reasonable exit, false imprisonment can have occurred. For example, in one famous case, a tow truck operator was in the process of jacking a car up when the owner came by. The owner offered to pay the operator but the operator replied that the owner would have to pick up her car at the tow lot. The owner got into the car and the tow operator proceeded to tow the car a few blocks with the owner in the car. The owner successfully sued the operator in a false imprisonment suit because all of the elements of false imprisonment had occurred.

Store owners must be careful with false imprisonment as this has been an issue when detaining suspected shoplifters. It is wise for business owners to seek out a business attorney with expertise in this area to provide guidance and procedures to avoid liability for this action.

Infliction of Emotional Distress

Infliction of emotional distress is extreme and outrageous conduct that causes severe emotional distress. This can be caused intentionally or recklessly. Infliction of emotional distress does not protect us from boorish behavior, rather it protects against extreme conduct that causes intense agony or mental pain. For example, some stalking crimes have been found to cause emotional distress to the point that they are actionable. A reasonable person can become so anxiety ridden that he or she can lose a job and be unable to function because of a stalker's behavior.

Defamation of Character

Not only can an individual be harmed physically and emotionally, the law recognizes that a person's reputation can be damaged by false statements. Despite our freedom of speech, that right does not extend to the point of injuring an individual's reputation and diminishing the respect he or she once had because of a lie told by another.

For defamation to occur one must make a false and defamatory statement about another that is communicated to a third party. Slander takes place when the statement is spoken orally. Libel takes place when the defamation is written, in the form of a picture, video or related medium.

Truth is a complete defense to defamation. Consequently, if someone repeats something about you that is embarrassing, but true, you will not be successful in a suit for defamation of character. There are also privileges which grant immunity from defamation liability.

Absolute privilege is granted in cases where statements are made by members of congress while on the floor of congress, statements made by participants in a judicial proceeding, and statements made between spouses when alone.

There is also a constitutional privilege to comment about public figures and public officials. In general we are allowed to criticize and comment about public figures and provided that our comments are not made with actual malice. If the comments are malicious, that is, if they are made with a clear reckless disregard for the truth, then a defamation suit will be successful. The idea of a free and unfettered debate in our society is one of our most important rights and the Supreme Court has reaffirmed that idea with regularity over the years. In effect, if you want the benefits of the public light, you must be willing to live with the headaches.

Invasion of Privacy

You may question how one could hold another accountable for comments made that are true, but embarrassing and private. This is the tort of invasion of privacy. Though the constitution does not explicitly guarantee the right to privacy, the supreme court has ruled that there is an implicit right of privacy in our society and we can reasonably expect to be "left alone" in the living of our lives.

Invasion of privacy can take place in the following ways:

- publishing private facts about an individual

- intruding on another's solitude

- appropriating another's name or likeness

- putting another in a false light

Private facts are things like medical records, grades from school etc. If a nurse in your doctor's office shares the fact that you have a loathsome disease or are seeing the physician for a sexual problem; that could be grounds for an invasion of privacy lawsuit.

We have the right to be left alone. That is, others do not have the right to intrude into our solitude. So regularly eavesdropping on someone's telephone conversations and similar types of actions can give rise to tort liability.

Individuals and businesses do not have the right to use our name or likeness for any reason (usually to sell a product or service) without our permission. For example, you may eat McDonalds hamburgers with regularity, but using you in a McDonald's ad without your permission is appropriation.

Publicizing something about another that puts him or her in a false light is one of the torts that fall under invasion of privacy. For example, a student newspaper publishing that a student is a member of a militia or the like when he is not could give rise to this tort. Additionally, the paper could also be sued for defamation.

Misuse of Legal Procedure

Using the legal process involves abuse of process, malicious prosecution and wrongful civil proceedings. This tort allows an injured party to collect damages in the event that another wrongfully institutes legal proceedings against him or her.

Torts Against Property

In addition to intentional torts against persons, we can be liable for torts against property as well. The most common property torts are discussed below:

Trespass to Real Property

Real property is defined as land or anything permanently affixed to the land. Personal property is defined as anything that is not real property. Crossing onto another's property, causing another individual to cross onto another's property, or causing an object to cross onto another's property without permission are all real property trespasses. If I cut across a neighbor's lawn, or I push a friend onto my neighbor's lawn or I throw a ball onto my neighbor's lawn and I have no permission from my neighbor, I am considered a trespasser. In general, the neighbor will have to prove damages, which in those examples would probably be difficult to prove. The damages can be in the form of a reduction in value of the land, loss of the property, and/or discomfort suffered by my neighbor as a result of my actions.

It should be recognized that many states have an "attractive nuisance" doctrine where if real property is considered 'inviting' to children; for example a swimming pool or a sand pile that would draw a child toward it, the landowner can be liable if a child is injured on the property despite being uninvited.

Nuisance

A real property nuisance takes place when one party interferes with the quiet enjoyment of another's property without being a trespasser. Smoke going from one parcel to another, or extremely loud music in a commercial shop that keeps customers from entering adjoining shops are both examples of real property nuisances.

Personal Property Trespass and Conversion

The unauthorized use or causing the dispossession of another's personal property is considered a trespass. If the act so damages the property or so interferes with the use of the property that it becomes nearly useless, then the act is considered conversion.

For example, if I hide your text from you for a couple of days and you experience some hardship for that time, I could be liable for personal property trespass. If I damage the book to where it us of no use, or keep it so long that you need a new text, then I am liable to you for conversion.

Fraudulent Misrepresentation (Deceit)

This is a tort that can come up in contractual relationships and is considered to be a harm to economic interests. The elements of fraud are:

> misrepresentation of facts with a knowledge of falsity or a reckless disregard for the truth

> intent to induce reliance by the party being defrauded

> justifiable reliance by the party being defrauded

> damages suffered by defrauded party

> cause of damages is the misrepresentation

Businesses must be careful in sales transactions to stay within the area of reasonable sales puffery (statements of opinion like "this is the best product for the money") and not misrepresent a product or service. For example, asserting that a car has new brakes or a new engine when it does not can give rise to the tort of fraud.

Interference with Contractual Relations

Another economic harm that can be suffered is when one party causes another involved in a contract not to perform that contract. For example, imagine that you are contracted to deliver 200 slabs of granite to a kitchen refinishing company at the end of this month. I am aware of your contract; and I induce you to sell me the granite and we both know that you will not be able to fulfil your contract with the kitchen refinishing company. In this example, I may be liable for interference with contractual relations.

Disparagement

Disparagement involves the making of a false statement that is published to a third party where the defendant knew the statement was false and did so with malicious intent. Products, services and business reputations can be disparaged. The tort is similar to defamation of character with similar defenses.

Negligence

As discussed earlier, torts can be committed intentionally, recklessly and negligently. (Later, we will discuss strict liability). Negligence occurs when we breach our duty of care to act like a reasonable person acting prudently and someone is injured or suffers damages because of our actions. To prove negligence in a lawsuit the plaintiff must prove the following:

A duty of care was owed to the plaintiff and it was breached by the defendant

The plaintiff suffered injury or damages

The injury or damages were proximately caused by the defendant's negligence

We all have a duty to act prudently and diligently as we go about our daily business whether it be personal or professional. We have a duty not to expose others to the risk of harm. We are judged in that duty based on a standard that is considered to be external and objective. Professionals are held to reasonability standards based on their superior knowledge or skill. Children and those who are physically disabled are held to standards of similar individuals who are like themselves in age, capability or experience. An individual who suffers from a mental deficiency is held to the standard of a reasonable person of a like standard who is not mentally deficient.

The classic example of negligence is the driving of a car. If you are distracted by the radio or a cell phone and injure someone in an accident; despite the fact that you did not intend to hurt anyone, you can be found to have been negligent and be liable for damages.

The area of business where negligence comes up with some unfortunate regularity is malpractice. Individuals who are licensed as physicians, attorneys, accountants and the like can be liable for malpractice if they do not follow the reasonable professional standards of their professions. You have probably read about medical, legal and accounting malpractice suits where it has been alleged that a professional breached his or her duty of care causing injury or damage for the plaintiff.

As a general rule, the law does not require that we act in another's behalf if someone is in peril. For example, you may walk by swimming pool and observe someone drowning. From a moral perspective most would contend that you should seek help for the victim or aid the victim yourself, but the law does not require that. You do have a duty if the victim is under your charge (you are the guardian or responsible for the victim in some way), or if you created the situation - you threw the victim in the pool. You also have a duty not to leave someone in greater peril than when you found him if you come to his aid. For example, you cannot begin to help a victim you find on the sidewalk who is unconscious, then leave the victim in the street where he could be hit by a car because you're late for an appointment. Outside of those areas we generally have no legal duty to aid another who is in trouble.

Some special negligence doctrines have been developed by the courts over the years for specific issues of negligence. One is the doctrine of "*res ipsa loquitur*," meaning "the thing speaks for itself". Under this concept, if a party has exclusive control of property or a situation where no injury would occur without negligence, the court permits the jury to infer negligent conduct and the causation of the injury. For example, you walk into a grocery store and a sign that hangs fifteen feet in the air drops on your head causing an injury. In this example, the store has exclusive control of the sign and it is reasonable to assume the store was negligent in that it fell.

Another doctrine to be aware of is *"negligence per se."* This takes place when a statute that was designed to protect members of the public is violated, and someone is injured, the court will hold that the defendant was negligent. For example, a driver who is convicted of exceeding the speed limit in his car who injures another in an accident may find herself civilly liable under negligence per se.

Avoiding Liability for Negligence

If we follow the duties of acting reasonably with diligence and prudence, we should be able to avoid liability for negligence lawsuits. While using common sense in many activities (like obeying all traffic laws when driving) may be sufficient to avoid some suits, there are specific duties we should be aware if we possess land.

We have a duty of care to virtually everyone who enters our property. A trespasser in general is not afforded much duty. However, we have a duty not to intentionally injure a trespasser. That means no setting traps that could injure or maim a trespasser.

Licensees and invitees on property are owed a duty of ordinary care meaning the owner must prevent injury or harm when an invitee or licensee comes onto the owner's property. As a minimum the property owner has a duty to warn those parties of conditions they would not likely discover on their own.

Limitations on Liability and Defenses to Negligence

In the case of an unforeseen consequence, one may avoid or reduce negligence liability in certain cases. For example, a driver may run a red light and collide with a truck carrying dynamite. The dynamite explodes. The driver of the truck is injured in the accident, and the driver of the car who created the situation will be liable for the injury to the truck driver. However, the blast breaks a store window two blocks away. The driver of the car will probably not be liable for the broken store window as it was not foreseeable.

Another way negligence liability can be limited is with a superseding cause. If I negligently injure you while I am pruning my tree by allowing a branch to drop on your head while you walk by, I am liable for that act. Imagine that I take you to the emergency room to have your head stitched as a result of the accident and the attending nurse negligently applies a compress causing an infection. I am not liable for the infection as the nurse's conduct was that of a superseding event. I will remain liable for the stitches to your head.

In situations where injury or damage has occurred because of alleged negligence by the defendant, there are defenses that may reduce or eliminate liability. One is risk assumption by the plaintiff. If the plaintiff consents to conduct that has an element of risk therein, the defendant may not be liable for negligence. For example, a college football player who breaks a leg during a routine practice will probably unsuccessful in suing the school for negligence because of the assumption of risk in playing football.

Comparative negligence is also a defense to negligence. Here, the plaintiff is negligent and therefore contributed to his or her own injury. In this case the courts measure the damages and reduce the award accordingly.

Strict Liability

Strict liability is liability without fault. One can be liable for injury or damage sustained by another despite the fact that the defendant did not act intentionally, recklessly or negligently. It has been determined over the years that some activities have so much risk of injury that the public should be able to collect for damages despite not having someone at fault. The types of activities involve abnormally dangerous activities like dynamite blasting, crop dusting, fumigation etc. These are activities that are not commonly engaged in everyday society. In addition, the keeping of wild animals can create strict liability for their owners. In general, individuals who keep wild animals do so almost entirely at their own risk because of the perceived public danger brought on by the animals.

We see strict liability in the way workmen's compensation insurance is administered in many states. With workmen's comp when a worker is injured on the job, no blame is assigned, rather the worker receives benefits per the agreement in the policy. On occasion, employers will get frustrated because an employee gets injured by not following certain safety precautions and is able to collect workmen's compensation. However, the good news for the employer is that in most cases if a worker is injured by an employer's negligence, the employer's workmen's compensation insurance protects the employer.

- product
- employment

36

Chapter 7

Contracts

"Agree, for the law is costly"- Thomas Fuller

Contracts are agreements that are the backbone of business. In American society most of us are involved in contracts on a regular basis. If you have purchased a good (like a cup of coffee) or a service (like getting a haircut) you have been involved in a contract. A contract is a legal agreement between two or more parties, supported by consideration that the law will enforce.

In an ideal world, contracts would not be needed. I would promise to purchase something from you for a price, you would deliver it on time and I would pay you. If there were a problem - a miscommunication of some kind, each of us, being perfect individuals would give the other party the benefit of the doubt and work the problem out. However, as we are well aware this is not a perfect world. We miscommunicate and some of us are less than honest. It is human nature to feel taken advantage of by others when things don't go our way, so we need the law to help ensure that our agreements are enforced.

Development of Contract Law

Contracts are a crucial element of business. The buying and selling of goods and services take place because parties contract with one another. Societies where business activity developed and expanded had to develop contract law. The ancient Egyptian societies had contract law as did the Mesopotamians. The Roman Empire held contracts very highly in their legal system with a great deal of formality being associated with certain types of agreements. Contract law became more complex and encompassed many elements of society in common law England as that society developed.

In the United States, we too, have gone through substantial changes in contracting as time has passed. You might remember that early in our history the United States had a philosophy of "laissez faire," meaning hands off, and the government that governs the least governs best. This was a time when most contracts- most business agreements- were done face to face. You might remember that we were primarily an agricultural economy for our first century or so. Consequently, the concept of *'caveat emptor'*, let the buyer beware, was an underlying philosophy in our method of contracting. We had what some have called "freedom of contract." We had the right to contract with whomever we wanted, to do whatever we agreed to. If one of the parties had more leverage than the other but both agreed to terms in a contract, the government did not step in and void the contract. This worked during the period that the average American grew up in a small agricultural village and most of the people he or she dealt with lived nearby.

Things began to change as the industrial revolution took place and the transcontinental railroad was built. As time passed we began to deal with mail order merchants who we never saw, we simply ordered goods from a catalog. The industrial revolution caused many citizens to leave the farm for the promise of work in the city. Society took on a different look and we began to demand more help from the government. The old adage "a deal is a deal" was pretty harsh for an individual who ordered something from a mail house two states away and the wrong product was shipped. The buyer in this case had no leverage, while the seller seemed to have it all.

The government began to regulate the economy more and contract law began to change. In the twentieth century merchants were scrutinized more closely. Administrative agencies began to expand in numbers and in regulatory power. Consumers were granted more protection in dealing with business. Workers were given rights that set a baseline for a contract. For example, in the 1930's congress passed the minimum wage. As you know, now it is illegal to contract with someone for less than the minimum wage. This is quite a difference from the laissez faire, let the buyer beware philosophy that pervaded the country less than one hundred and fifty years ago. We have moved from what some have called the "classical period" of contracting to the modern era where the government has a greater voice in contracting than in the past.

Elements of a Contract

For a contract to be binding, there are four essential elements it must have. If the contract is missing one element, there is no contract. The four elements are:

> Mutual Assent - the parties must agree
>
> Consideration - both parties must give something up
>
> Legality - the contract must concern legal matters
>
> Capacity - both parties must be legally capable

Mutual Assent

A contract begins with an agreement. Both parties must agree unequivocally on the subject matter and terms of the contract. For example, you stop by a coffee shop to buy a cup of coffee. You want coffee, the shop wants to sell it to you. The price is $1.90. You agree on the price. You must pay immediately to get the coffee. The shop must deliver the coffee immediately. Both parties agree to the subject matter and the terms of the contract. Enjoy the coffee and try not to spill it.

Consideration

Both parties must give up something of legal sufficiency. In the example above, you give up your hard earned $1.90 and the shop gives up its valuable coffee. In essence you have bargained for the price and given something up in exchange. You receive a legal benefit in getting the coffee, and you are detrimented in having to pay the $1.90

Legality

The courts will not enforce agreements that are illegal. Coffee is a legal product and the payment of cash is an acceptable form of payment in our society. If you were contracting to purchase an illegal drug like cocaine or heroine, you paid the money that had been agreed upon and the seller did not deliver the drugs, it would be rather difficult to get the court to enforce your contract. Contracts have to be legal to have the law enforce them.

Capacity

Both you and the shop attendant must be capable of understanding the terms and performance of the contract. If one of the parties is incapable, then there can be no mutual assent. For example, the author used to contract with his daughters (in writing in their baby books!) that in exchange for some gum or candy when grocery shopping the girls had to agree to not date until they were twenty-five years old and they had to begin paying their father $1000.00 per month when they began making $100,000.00 per year. This was agreed to when the girls were two and four years of age. Obviously, they did not understand the terms of the agreement and (unfortunately) the courts would never hold them to it. Both parties must comprehend the subject matter and terms of the agreement. We will discuss minor's rights later. In fact minor children can contract and have some protections that can make businesses shiver.

Contract Law

Contracts are governed primarily by state common law. In many instances, state common law is displaced by the Uniform Commercial Code (UCC) in the sale of tangible personal property. The UCC is statutory law that governs sales transactions of personal property. The UCC (also referred to as the Code) has been around for over one hundred years and has been implemented by all fifty states (except for Louisiana, which has adopted part of the UCC). The UCC provides a uniform set of rules to govern commercial sales transactions. It was recognized when the Code was first envisioned that each state had its own common law of contracting. The laws were not exactly alike which could create problems for the easy movement of goods from state to state. The UCC was developed with this in mind. Article 2 of the code expressly applies only to contracts for the sale of goods. The UCC does not apply to real estate contracts, employment contracts or contracts for intangibles like patents and copyrights.

Classification of Contracts

Contracts can be classified into how they are formed, what stage of performance they are in, and similar ways. The following are brief discussions of basic contract classification:

Bilateral and Unilateral Contracts

Bilateral contracts are contracts where there has been an exchange of two promises. For example, I promise to pay you $25 if you promise to cut my lawn on Saturday. Notice that there are two promises. I am looking for a commitment from you before any performance begins. We agree and both parties are bound.

In a unilateral contract there is a promise for an act. A classic example of a unilateral contract is a reward. You are waiting to board a bus and see an advertisement for a reward on a telephone pole offering $50 for a lost dog named Fluffy. You see the dog near to the bus stop. If you return the dog the owner must pay you the $50, however, you are not bound or committed to return the dog. You can choose to board the bus, ignore the dog and hope that Fluffy is not hit by a car. This is a promise for an act, a unilateral contract.

Express and Implied Contracts

Express contracts are contracts where the terms are expressed orally, in writing or both. For example, earlier when you walked into the coffee shop to purchase coffee, imagine that there is a sign indicating that the coffee you want is $1.90. This is an express term.

An implied contract is a contract where actions deem that mutual assent has occurred and a contract is formed. For example, you are waiting in line at a hot dog stand. The stand does not show prices of any kind. While waiting in line, you take a bag of chips from the stand, open it and begin eating the chips. You have made an implied promise to pay for those chips despite not knowing what the price may be.

Valid, Unenforceable, Voidable, Void Contracts

A valid contract is a contract that the law will enforce. It has all of the essential elements of a contract and is therefore binding on both parties.

An unenforceable contract is a contract that cannot be enforced by the courts for some reason. The reason may be that it is a special kind of contract requiring evidence of writing to be enforced (not all contracts need a writing for enforceability). Or the period of time for enforcement, the statute of limitations, has run out.

A voidable contract is a contract where one or both parties has the legal right to cancel the contract for some reason. For example, we agree that I shall purchase your house for $400,000 within 60 days, contingent or conditioned upon my ability to get 7% fixed rate financing. If I am not able to get the financing, I have the right to cancel the contract. Another example is where one party has defrauded another (remember the tort of fraud?). The defrauded party has the right to cancel the contract if he or she so chooses.

A void contract is a contract that is missing one of the essential four elements. It lacks mutual assent, consideration, legality or capacity. For example, an illegal agreement, an agreement to purchase stolen property, is a void contract because it lacks legality.

Executed and Executory Contracts

An executed contract is one where all of the parties have performed their contractual duties. In the example of the coffee purchase, you have received your coffee and the shop has been paid.

An executory contract is one where the duties have not been finished. There is an agreement and until all duties are finished, the contract is executory.

Quasi-Contractual Obligations

There are a couple of areas where despite the lack of a contract or the lack of one of the elements of a contract, a party may still be bound to perform as if there was a contract in place. The first non-contractual obligations deal with unjust enrichment. In certain situations, if a party is unjustly enriched by another party, the enriched party will have to provide consideration for the enrichment. This is called quasi-contract. If one party provides a benefit and the other party knowingly accepts it, the benefited party will have to pay for the benefit. For example, gardeners come into your neighborhood and have contracted to cut your neighbor's lawn. This is their first time in the area and they make a mistake and begin to cut your lawn. You see what they are doing and do not stop them. In this case, you are knowingly being unjustly enriched and will be liable to pay them under the doctrine of quasi-contract.

The other area where one will be required to perform despite the lack of a contract is promissory estoppel. If I induce you to detriment yourself by promising something in return, though we may not have a contract, I may be forced to provide consideration. A well-known example of promissory estoppel is where A promises B a job. B quits her existing job; shows up at A's place of business and A does not come through with the job as promised. Here we have a promise that induced reliance and an injustice will result if A does not perform. B will be able to rely on the doctrine of promissory estoppel for damages in this case.

Finally, there is the issue of charitable subscriptions. If a charity is promised consideration (usually a monetary donation) by a donor, and the donor does not perform, the charity can force payment if it can prove that it relied upon the promise. For example, after you get out of college you become very successful and promise your school a $3,000,000.00 donation over three years. You pay the first year but choose not to the next two years. If the school can prove it relied on the promised amounts (it has begun a building project or something like that) it will be able to collect the amount based on the charitable subscription concept.

Chapter 8

Offer, Acceptance, Invalid Assent

"Ancient custom has the force of law" – Legal Maxim

The first element needed in forming a contract is mutual assent. Both parties must agree unequivocally on the subject matter and terms of the agreement. Mutual assent is usually a two step process. The first step is making an offer, the second step is accepting the offer.

In order for an offer to be valid it must have three components. It must be communicated, it must be definite and certain and it must manifest an intent to contract. If one of those elements is missing, it cannot be considered a valid offer. The person making the offer is called the offeror and the person receiving the offer is the offeree. You will find in law that in most cases the giver of something has an 'or' at the end of the term and the receiver of something has a 'ee' at the end of the term. For example, a landlord who rents property is referred to as the lessor and the person who rents the property, the tenant, is referred to as the lessee. The landlord gives over the property and the tenant receives the property in a contractual relationship.

Communication

For an offer to be communicated, the offeror must make the offer or have an agent do so. (An agent is someone you appoint or authorize to do something on your behalf). It has to be clear that the offeror directed the agent to make the offer. For example, imagine that you are considering selling your car to a friend who you know is very interested in buying it. While sitting at your desk you write the following: "I hereby offer to sell my 1973 Dodge Dart to my good friend Ray D. Aiter for a cash price of $500.00." You put the offer in an envelope with Ray's name on it and leave on your desk in your dorm room at school. During the day you do some research and find that the car is actually worth $1500.00, so you're glad that you never sent the offer to Ray. While you are at school working on your Business Law course, the maintenance person who cleans the dorms sees the envelope with Ray's name on it, happens to know Ray, picks it up and delivers the letter to him. Ray sees you later that day and says, "I accept." Do you have a contract? At this point you do not because the offer was never communicated. You did not intend to communicate the offer, and you never authorized the maintenance person to act on your behalf.

Offers can be made to one or a few specific parties, or an offer can be made to the general public. In any event, the offeree must be aware of the offer in order to accept it.

Definite and Certain

The offer must be definite and certain enough so that a court (a neutral third party) can determine what was offered and give an appropriate remedy to the offeree if the offeror does not perform. This means the terms must be clear enough so that a party can accept and with that acceptance have a contract. An offer can have open terms, but again, there must be sufficient information about what is being offered so that the offeree can say "I accept," which creates a contract. For example, it is common in the produce industry for an offer to be made that looks like this:

5 tons of red flame grapes at December 03 market price to be delivered on or before 12/31/03. Payment terms net 30.

Here a grower is offering to sell produce at a price to be specified in December 2003. Despite the fact that the price is unknown until that time, the offer is still definite enough to be accepted and thus create a contract.

Contrast that offer with advertising circulars that come to your home. Many are held not to be offers because they are not definite and certain enough to be considered an offer. Many terms (like quantity availability and payment terms) are left off. In a substantial number of cases those advertisements are held to be invitations to negotiate.

Manifest an Intent to Contract

The offer must exhibit an objective intent to contract in order to be valid. This means that a reasonable third party who is not a part of the transaction, watching what has transpired would contend that the offeror intends to contract. Offers made in jest, anger and the like are not considered to manifest an intent to contract if a reasonable third party could understand, given the circumstances, that the offeror wasn't serious.

Businesses are involved in and encounter issues of offers that make an understanding as to how an offer is made important. For example, auctions are invitations seeking offers, not offers themselves. If an auction is made with reserve, the auctioneer reserves the right to withdraw the item being auctioned if the offers made are not high enough. If an auction is made without reserve, the auction must sell to the highest bidder.

Often businesses will seek offers to create competition among suppliers and arrive at the most favorable terms for a project or expensive item. It is common in construction projects to issue a request for proposal or request for quotation (RFP, RFQ) asking different suppliers to bid on a job. This allows the purchaser to determine the best price and terms, without necessarily committing to anyone on the project. Here, the purchaser is an offeree, not an offeror.

Offer Termination

Once an offer is made, how long does it remain valid? If your first thought is it stays valid for a reasonable period of time, you're on the right track. There are several ways that an offer is terminated. Each is discussed below:

Revocation

In general, an offeror can revoke/withdraw his or her offer at anytime. There are a few exceptions to this rule, but for the most part, the offeror is the master of the offer. For example, you might offer to sell some furniture at a garage sale and after a few hours decide to keep the furniture and take it off the market. You may do so because no one has accepted your offer. You must however, communicate your revocation to the offeree(s). For example, I make an offer in the student newspaper to pay $100 to the first person to bring me an original cabbage patch doll. If I decide to revoke the offer, I must advertise the revocation in the newspaper. Putting a sign up on my door in the dorm would not be an effective revocation.

Exceptions to Revocation

There are certain offers that cannot be revoked. Option contracts cannot be revoked because a party has given the offeror consideration to keep an offer open. An option contract works like this: I offer to sell a certain plot of land for $200,000. You offer to pay me $2000 to keep the offer open to you for another two weeks. I accept the $2000 and agree to those terms. If you do not exercise your option to purchase the land, I keep the money and do what I want with the land after the two weeks have passed. If you exercise your option during the two week period, I must sell you the land for $200,000 as we agreed. I do not have the right to revoke that offer during those two weeks because you paid me to keep the offer open.

A unilateral contract where the offeree has begun performance cannot be revoked and the offeree must be given a reasonable time to perform. For example, I make an offer to pay $500 to the first business law student who completely cuts the grass on the football field with a hand mower. You start to work and when you are 80% complete I revoke my offer. Obviously, that would not be reasonable. I must permit you a reasonable time to finish the job.

A firm offer under the UCC cannot be revoked during its offer period as well. A firm offer is an offer made in writing by a merchant who gives a signed writing assurance that the offer will not be revoked during its offer period. If no time limit is stated on the offer then it terminates after a reasonable time and no longer than three months from the offer date. For example, XYZ Suppliers offer to sell processed rubber at a price of 5 cents per pound to ABC Tire Stores for a period of three weeks. XYZ cannot revoke the offer during those three weeks. If XYZ had not set a termination date on the offer then it would have been open for no longer than three months. If XYZ was offering to sell processed milk instead of rubber and the milk has a shelf life of two weeks and no termination date was given, then the offer would terminate after a reasonable time. In this case a reasonable time would be two weeks or less.

Time Lapse

An offeror can specify the length of time that an offer is open. After that period the offer is terminated. If the offeror does not specify the termination date, the offer will terminate after a reasonable period of time. Circumstances of the subject matter of the offer, industry practices, past performance etc., help determine a reasonable time period in those cases.

Rejection and Counteroffer

When an offeree rejects the offer, it is terminated. The offeree must communicate the rejection because any offer terminates after a period of time. But when the offeree expressly rejects an offer the offer is off the table and unavailable to the offeree.

A counteroffer operates as a rejection and a new offer. If goods or services are being offered at one price and the offeree offers to pay less than the offer on the table, the original offer is rejected and the offeree becomes an offeror.

Recognize that requests for information do not operate as a rejection or a counteroffer. Questions like, *"Is that your best price?"* or *"Would you accept a lower price for a cash sale?"* are not rejections. Rather, the offeree in this example is trying to gain as much information as possible about the offer. Effective negotiators understand that information requests can be very effective in determining favorable price, terms etc.

Recognize that a conditional acceptance is a counteroffer. For example, I offer to sell you my house for $300,000. You accept conditioned upon my painting the outside of the house. You have not accepted a mirror image of my offer. You have made a counteroffer that increases my burden if I accept it.

Incompetency and Death

If the offeror or offeree become incompetent or dies during the offer period the offer is terminated. Incompetence means that one of the parties can no longer comprehend the offer being made. Both death and incompetence terminate an offer.

Subsequent Illegality

If the offer becomes illegal during the offer period, the offer is terminated. For example, State A allows fireworks to be purchased during June and July of every year. In January of the current year, Big Blast fireworks offers to sell 20 tons of fireworks for $100,000 to XYZ Stores in State A. In February of that same year State A outlaws fireworks. The offer by Big Blast to XYZ is terminated.

Destruction of Subject Matter

If the subject matter of the offer is destroyed, the offer is terminated. I offer to sell you my car for $5000, you say you will think about it and let me know within one week. The car is wrecked during the week before you decide to accept. The offer is terminated. Next time don't dawdle!

Acceptance

Assuming that the offer negotiates the minefield of termination possibilities listed above, the offer must be accepted in order for a contract to be formed. For acceptance to be valid it must be unequivocal and it must be communicated to the offeror. Unequivocal acceptance is what is referred to as the mirror image rule. What is offered is what is accepted, simple as that.

How does one accept unequivocally? If your first thought was in some reasonable fashion, you're remaining on the right track. There are some specifics that govern valid acceptance.

Silence

In general, silence is not a reasonable way to accept an offer. Obviously, there is little communication in silence. However, there are some exceptions to silence not being an effective acceptance. If the parties have a past practice of silence meaning consent then silence can accept an offer. For example, ABC is a farmer who grows lettuce. ABC has done business with XYZ Distributing for several years. The two parties have agreed that ABC calls nightly by 8PM to offer the daily crop and does so by leaving the offer on XYZ's answering machine. If XYZ does NOT call by midnight, then the offer is accepted and XYZ picks up its goods the following morning. Because the two parties have a past practice history with one another and do business in this fashion, silence will constitute acceptance.

You might remember earlier in the study guide that the doctrine of quasi-contract may make a party liable for something that was not agreed to. This can happen in unilateral agreements. For example, you witness a gardener mistakenly begin to cut your lawn and choose not to stop him.

Your silence could be implied as acceptance of his performance and you might be liable to pay a reasonable value for the service.

Authorized Means

Acceptance must take place in a reasonable manner (as one might expect). Utilizing the same or faster means as employed in the offer is considered a reasonable way to accept. For example, if the offer is made in writing and comes by first class mail, acceptance in writing by first class mail would generally be acceptable.

If the offer requires a specific mode of acceptance, such as filling out a form etc., then a valid acceptance requires conformance to that specification. Accepting in another fashion constitutes a counteroffer which the original offeror can accept or reject.

Acceptance is generally effective upon dispatch and rejection is effective upon receipt. This can cause some problems when one party rejects and then later tries to accept an offer. The general rule here is that whichever communication arrives to the offeror first will determine whether or not a contract is made. For example, you receive an offer in the mail from a supplier offering to sell you 1000 pounds of fertilizer for $500. You write "Reject" on the form and send it back in the postage paid, first class envelope on Monday, 7/1. On Tuesday, 7/2 you decide that the offer is a good one and would like to accept. You fax your order to the supplier that day and the supplier receives your fax before the rejection. There is a contract. If the supplier received your rejection before receiving your fax, there would be no contract.

In general, when a party accepts an offer, a contract is formed at that instant. Following up with a writing evidences that the contract exists unless one of the parties makes the writing a condition of the contract.

UCC Battle of the Forms

While common law requires a mirror image acceptance to an offer to create a contract, the UCC is a little more liberal in dealing with the rules of acceptance. There is a recognition that merchants often have numerous terms and conditions as part of their standard purchase order or order acknowledgement forms. A buyer will typically have terms that are favorable to the buyer and the seller will have favorable seller's terms. When a buyer places an order and the seller accepts the order, the terms and conditions of the two parties are different, therefore lacking a mirror image. If the primary terms of the contract are agreed to (such as price, terms of delivery, payment, etc.), and if the offeree does not expressly state that acceptance is conditioned or contingent upon acceptance of the additional terms and conditions, the code holds that a contract exists. The UCC focuses on the intent of the parties in the battle of the forms.

Invalid Assent

Mutual assent is one of the key elements of a contract. We have discussed assent in focusing on the offer and acceptance. The word mutual is just as important in mutual assent as is the word assent. Both parties in a contract must freely enter into the contract without being forced by another party. Moreover, in some cases involving a mistake that both parties make, the contract may be voidable.

There are several actions that can cause a contract to be voidable or void. They are discussed below:

Fraud in the Inducement

As discussed earlier in torts, fraud is an area where businesses can have trouble because the sales function can lend itself to fraud in certain situations. Fraud in the inducement involves a material misrepresentation (a falsity) of fact that induces another to enter into a contract. For fraud in inducement to occur the following must be present:

> misrepresentation of facts with a knowledge of falsity or a reckless disregard for the truth

> intent to induce reliance by the party being defrauded

> justifiable reliance by the party being defrauded

In fraud in the inducement one party deceives the other with a false statement to persuade the other party to enter into a contract. For example, you are considering buying my car and state that gas mileage is very important to you because you do a lot of driving as part of your job. I tell you that the gas mileage on the car I'm selling runs at 30 miles to the gallon. It actually gets 18 miles to the gallon and has never gotten close to 30 miles to the gallon. My statement, should you rely upon it, could be grounds for voiding the agreement. Fraud in the inducement makes the contract voidable at the option of the defrauded party. Moreover, it can lead to tort liability for the party who perpetrated the fraud.

In general, one party does not have the duty to point out defects to the other party prior to the contract agreement. For example, the brakes on my car may only have 1000 miles left before a brake job is needed. I do not necessarily have to disclose that, however, I cannot lie and say the car has new brakes - that would be fraud in the inducement.

Additionally, concealment of a defect is considered fraud in most cases. If I put an extra heavy engine oil into the car to conceal a knock, that could create a grounds for fraud and allow you to void the contract.

There are certain areas where defects must be disclosed. For instance, in selling California owner occupied real estate, sellers have a duty to disclose all known defects before selling.

A contract where one party has innocently misrepresented a fact is grounds for voidability by the other party. For example, I am selling you a commercial space in an office. You state that you need a minimum of 1500 square feet for your business. I am confident that the space is at least that, however, I do not measure the footage and the space turns out to be 1200 square feet. The agreement is voidable by you.

Fraud in the Execution

This type of fraud makes a contract void because there is no mutual assent. It should be mentioned that fraud in the execution is difficult to pull off and consequently rarely seen in business. It takes place when one party misrepresents to the other the nature of a document that represents the contract. For example, you contract to pay an accountant $500 per month to provide certain accounting services for your company, but as you are getting ready to sign the contract, the accountant drops something on the floor and persuades you to pick it up. While your are picking it up, she changes the document and you sign a contract stating you will pay $5000 per month for the agreed services. This agreement is void.

Duress and Undue Influence

Contracts that are not freely agreed to are void or voidable. In the event that a party agrees to a contract because of the threat of physical force, the agreement is void. In the event that an improper threat induces a party into a contract, the agreement is voidable by the party who is threatened.

For example, I induce you to purchase my car by explaining that if you don't I will tell your wife that you have been unfaithful to her. This agreement is voidable at your option, because of my exerting mental duress.

In the event that one party has a dominant relationship over another and improperly utilizes that relationship to induce the other party into a contract, that agreement is voidable as well. This is the use of undue influence. For example, your teacher implies that you will receive a bad grade unless you purchase her car. That contract is voidable at your option.

Unilateral and Mutual Mistake

Generally, when one party makes a mistake about a contract, he or she is not allowed to void the agreement. For example, I look at several computer systems at a computer store. I am interested in having sound as part of the computer system, but mistakenly choose a computer without sound. The order is written up and I take the system home and use it. In the absence of the computer store allowing for free returns for a certain period of time, I will probably not be able to void the contract. Ordinary risks of business are not grounds for voiding a contract. I sell stock in a company at $35 per share thinking it will not go any higher. You purchase the stock and it runs to $60 per share. I have no grounds for voiding the contract despite my mistake. There are some exceptions however, to the unilateral mistake rule.

If the other party is aware of my mistake and takes advantage of it, that is grounds for voiding the contract. A unilateral mistake made because of a clerical error that can be proven is grounds for voiding a contract as well.

Mutual mistake of material fact by both parties renders an agreement voidable by the adversely affected party unless she bears the risk of the mistake. For example, a bookkeeper agrees to provide payroll services for a local firm at the price of $150 per month for a local firm in a state where there is minimal state tax filing requirements. The firm has several out of state employees, which will require out of state filing beyond the area of expertise of the bookkeeper and more work than is bid upon. The firm believes the bid covers all filing required by the several states. In this example, there has been a mutual mistake of material fact and the contract is voidable.

Chapter 9

Consideration

"The last benefit is the one remembered" – Barber, *The Book of 1000 Proverbs*

Part of establishing objective intent in a contract is determining what the two parties have provided one another and what they have given up in a contract. This is the concept of consideration. Valid consideration must be legally sufficient and it must be bargained for and given in exchange for other consideration when contracting.

For legal sufficiency the promisee must be detrimented or the promisor must receive a legal benefit. A detriment occurs when the promisee agrees to do something he or she was not required to do before contracting. A benefit occurs when the promisor receives something he or she had no right to before contracting. An example of an agreement where both parties are detrimented is a contract where you agree to give up drinking alcoholic beverages for the period of two months in exchange for your brother paying you $500. By giving up drinking you are giving up something you have a legal right to do (even though it might be good for you to stop drinking). You are detrimented. Your brother is detrimented as well in that he must give up $500 if you fulfil your part of the bargain. You also receive a legal benefit. You are entitled to money that you were not entitled to before. You might make the argument your brother receives the benefit of knowing you're not going to call him at midnight asking for rides home from a bar.

Be careful in recognizing the concept of adequacy in consideration. Often, we think adequacy means that consideration must be fair. This is not necessarily the case. As long as both parties give something up, in general, consideration will be adequate. Sometimes an extreme difference in the value of consideration can cause one of the other elements to be questioned. For instance, there was a case several years ago when a teenage friend of the author's was able to purchase a brand new bicycle for $10 from another teenager. The bike turned out to be stolen. Paying $10 for a $500 item gave rise to questions such as whether there was true mutual assent (possible duress), if both parties were capable, or if the contract was legal. In the bicycle case, the agreement was illegal.

Illusory Promises

Sometimes one of the most effective ways to determine if consideration is present is to recognize what is not considered to be consideration. For example, for a contract to be valid both parties must provide consideration. In the case of an illusory promise, only one party is bound. An example is where I promise to purchase from you all of the flowers I wish from your flower stand over the next year. You may think that you need to stock up on more flowers than you might originally have planned because of my promise. But I am not committing to anything. I might want twelve dozen roses per month or I may not want any. You are bound, but I am not. My commitment is an illusion, I am not detrimented.

Do not confuse illusory promises with output and requirement contracts. Under the code, two parties can agree to provide output or requirements and meet consideration requisites. For instance, I own a Christmas tree farm and can harvest between 2000 and 2200 trees in a given season. You can sell up to 3000 of my trees, so you contract to purchase all of my output. It should be mentioned that I cannot go out and purchase another farm and deliver 6000 trees to you (unless we agree to that). Reasonability is considered in all cases. Imagine the same scenario but you can only sell between 800 and 1000 trees. I contract to provide all of the trees you require. This is a valid contract. In both cases we must act in good faith with one another.

Preexisting Obligations

As a general rule, if a party has a preexisting duty to do something it does not satisfy the requirement of consideration. We all have an existing obligation not to commit torts and crimes. If you and I form a contract where I agree not to batter you for the next two months in exchange for your payment of $100, that agreement is not valid. I already have a duty not to injure you and the agreement obviously violates public policy as well.

Public officials such as police officers, firemen and firewomen have a preexisting duty to protect the public. If I offer a police officer $200 per month for extra vigilance around my store while she walks her beat, the contract fails the test of consideration. She has a preexisting obligation to do the best job she can in protecting the public.

Modifications to Contracts

A preexisting contractual duty also fails the test of consideration. For example, imagine you hire XYZ Contractors to do a room addition to your house at a price of $50,000. During the construction the contractor explains that he underbid the job and needs an additional $5,000 to finish on time. You are not happy, but agree to pay the additional amount. The contractor provides nothing more than what was in the original contract and finishes on time. The contractor has provided no additional consideration and under common law would not be able to collect the additional $5,000. If both parties agreed to substitute a new contract for the old one, or if you both agreed on some additional work the contractor would do, then the additional amount could be collected. This is what is referred to as a modification of a contract at common law. The Restatement does allow for modifications without additional consideration if circumstances are different than when the contract was made.

Under the Code, if both parties agree to a modification in good faith, despite lack of additional consideration by one of the parties, then the modification is enforceable. For instance, you order a new television set from Circuit City at a price of $900. Before the set is delivered you see that Circuit City drops the advertised price to $750. You call Circuit City and demand the lower price and the store agrees to the change. Despite the fact you are already under contract and you are providing no additional consideration in the agreement, the modification is enforceable. This is a modification under the Code.

Liquidated and Unliquidated Debts

If two parties contract and agree on a price for an item or service the debt associated with the contract is liquidated or undisputed. That debt must be paid in full if the product or service is tendered according to the contract. For example, you contract with ABC Plumbing to clean a drain in your house for $75. ABC cleans the drain quickly and sends you the bill. You feel that the price is high given the amount of time ABC was at your house. You send ABC a check for $45 and state that the check is for payment in full and that upon cashing the check ABC loses all rights for additional payment. Because you and ABC have an undisputed, liquidated debt, ABC will be able to collect the remaining $30 from you. You have a preexisting legal obligation in this example.

If a debt is unliquidated (disputed); that is a price was never agreed to, then partial payment may satisfy the debt. Take the previous example with the plumber. If you and ABC had never discussed a price, you simply agreed that ABC would unclog the drain and send you a bill, then a partial payment can satisfy the debt. In the event that you sent the $45 and stated that this was a full payment then if ABC cashed the check you would be relieved of further liability. You must honestly dispute the amount, and you are liable for a reasonable value of the goods or services provided.

An accord and satisfaction is also available when a contracted amount is disputed. An accord is an agreement for one party to accept something other than that which was originally agreed upon. The satisfaction of the accord takes place when the consideration is provided. For example, a contractor provides services to you and bills you $1000. You disagree with the amount. You offer to pay $500 and provide the contractor your old computer system to settle the debt. The contractor agrees to your proposal. The different terms offered and agreed upon are the accord, when you pay the money and deliver the computer system the accord is satisfied.

Composition Agreements and Bankruptcy

There are situations where an undisputed debt can be discharged for less than full payment. A composition agreement is where all creditors agree to accept a certain percentage of amounts owed in order to avoid a debtor's bankruptcy. For instance, ABC owes your firm $5,000. ABC calls you and several other suppliers together and states the company has fallen on hard times and is going out of business. There are debts to suppliers in the amount of $100,000. The company has $60,000 available to pay its creditors. If all creditors agree to accept 60% of what is owed, then a composition agreement is in force, and paying less than the undisputed debt will be enforceable. ABC will not have to pay the remaining 40% it owes its creditors.

If a company goes bankrupt, the court will specify how much each creditor will receive. That too will allow a company to pay less than the contracted amount of an undisputed debt and be relieved from further liability.

Agreements Lacking Consideration

Generally past consideration and moral obligations do not meet the criteria for consideration in a contract. Past consideration works like this. Your company is supposed to receive 1000 bicycles by December 1 of the current year for a price of $120,000. Your supplier has run into trouble and requests to be allowed to deliver the bikes on December 10. Additionally, the supplier asks to be paid in full because it is currently struggling. Though the late date will cause a few problems you agree because the you have a good relationship with the supplier and would like to continue to do business with him. The supplier delivers the bicycles on December 10, and you pay him the $120,000. In February of the following year you owe the supplier $40,000 on a separate contract for bicycle parts. The payment is due February 15. You have a cash flow problem and ask your supplier to allow you to pay six weeks late on March 30. The supplier does not agree and states he needs his money when due. You might remind him of your generosity when he needed your help, but that is past consideration. There is no bargained for exchange in this second example. You will not be able to force your supplier to modify the second contract to allow you to pay later.

Gratuitous promises are generally not enforceable. If one party promises to do something for another with no exchange of consideration, the agreement lacks bargained for exchange and fails the test of consideration. For instance, you promise your next door neighbor to cut her lawn every week when you cut your own. The first week you cut your lawn and then run out of gas and fail to cut your neighbor's. The second week you cut your lawn but are in a hurry to go out and fail to cut your neighbor's lawn again. Will the neighbor be successful in suing you for not cutting her lawn? She has provided no consideration, there was no bargained for exchange, so your promise is unenforceable.

You might remember that the doctrine of promissory estoppel applies to promises that meet the following requirements:

Promise made

Justifiably relied upon

An injustice will occur to promisee because of the detriment suffered

The example given earlier was one where an individual quits a job to take another and the new job offer is withdrawn. Another area where promissory estoppel is seen is in the granting of franchises. From time to time, franchisers promise to reduce or waive a fee to a prospective franchisee if the franchisee will purchase property in a specific location and develop it to certain standards. If the franchiser then refuses to reduce or waive the fee, franchisees have been successful in suing under the doctrine of promissory estoppel.

Chapter 10

Legality and Capacity

"Honesty is the best policy" – Miguel de Cervantes

As discussed earlier, a contract must concern legal matters in order for it to be enforceable in court. The law would be in an impossible situation if it had to enforce illegal agreements. Consequently, the courts take a very dim view of individuals who are involved in illegality. They tend to take a harsh approach following the idea of "in pari delicto" with the parties who are involved in illegal agreements. "In pari delicto" means at equal fault and the court tends to leave the parties where they stand if they seek the court's help in dealing with an illegal agreement.

The courts will not enforce violations of statutes such as contracts to commit crimes or torts and it would be rare indeed, that anyone would come to court expecting help when he or she contracted to do anything illegal. Examples of these would be contracts that corrupt public officials through the use of bribes and similar actions. The courts will not help the parties in such agreements.

Gambling laws are one example of how courts will not aid parties in statute violations. Wagering is illegal in virtually all states with some notable exceptions. Two obvious exceptions to gambling illegality are state run lotteries and regulated gambling allowed by statute such as that seen at horse races and casinos in certain states. Wagering outside of those arenas is illegal and the courts will not help an individual collect a bet. For example, you bet your best friend that the Yankees will win the World Series. Your friend chooses the Giants. The Yankees win in six games. You come to collect your bet and your friend says he will never pay you. Don't bother going to court to enforce the agreement, it is illegal.

Sometimes risk shifting contracts are perceived as wagering contracts, but there is a difference between the two. Risk shifting contracts are insurance contracts. Generally there is no problem with insurance contracts provided that one party involved in such an agreement has an insurable interest. For example, if you and I hardly know each other, it is not reasonable that I have insurance on your car. If you get in an accident, I get paid. In that example, it appears that I have a vested interest in you having an accident. You on the other hand have good reason to insure your car and to avoid accidents; you have an insurable interest.

Licensing Statutes

All states have several licensing statutes designed to protect the public and to raise revenue. Those statutes that require competency through education, testing, good moral character and/or financial responsibility such as those required for a medicine, law, accounting, general contracting etc. are called regulatory licenses. If an individual contracts to do something for which she lacks a regulatory license, she will not be able to collect for the value of the services. For example, Josephine holds herself out to be a licensed general contractor and contracts to do remodeling services that require a license. She finishes the job and the client discovers she has no license and chooses not to pay her. She will be unsuccessful in suing for payment because she requires a regulatory license to do the work she contracted to do.

Contrast regulatory licenses with revenue raising licenses. A revenue raising license is a license that is in place to raise revenue for a government agency and not in place for public protection purposes. Typically the courts will allow a party to collect for services rendered despite the lack of a revenue raising license. An example is a fishing license where no competency or training is required. One simply pays a fee and receives the license. A wilderness guide who contracts to take a party on a camping trip where fishing is done and lacks a fishing license would be able to collect for his services if the party refused to pay.

Usury Laws/Public Policy

Usury laws apply to the lending of money. A usury statute sets the highest rate at which a lender may charge for loaning money. The rates vary from state to state and many lenders are exempt from usury laws. For example, institutional lenders such as banks, insurance companies and savings banks are exempt from most usury laws. If a lender who falls under usury laws violates the usury rate he or she may be liable to forfeit the excess interest that exceeded the usury rate, or in some cases forfeit all of the interest earned.

The courts will not enforce contracts that are contrary to public policy. Examples of these contracts are restraint of trade, unconscionable agreements, and those that excuse a party from its own negligence and the like. The courts tend to leave the parties where they stand in an agreement that violates public policy and usually do not offer redress to those involved in such contracts. However, there are some exceptions to courts not enforcing such agreements or aiding parties who are part of such contracts. Those contracts are summarized below.

Ignorance of Fact

If one of the parties is ignorant of a fact that makes an agreement illegal, in some cases the courts will aid the ignorant party. For example, I contract to sing at your nightclub for the month of January. I am unaware of the fact that you no longer have a performance license allowing singing at your club. At the end of the month after I have performed you inform me you have no license and will not pay me because the lack of a license makes the agreement illegal. The courts will help me in this case because it was reasonable for me to assume that you have a performance license.

Restraint of Trade

Typically, an agreement that limits or restrains trade violates public policy as well as some statutes. Certain employment contracts and contracts to sell a business actually call for restraint of trade as a term for one of the parties to follow. These agreements are acceptable provided that the terms are not the primary purpose of the contract, and the restraint is reasonable. For example, if you work as a design engineer for IBM, it is likely that you are not allowed to work for a competitor during the term of your employment, and possibly for six months thereafter. Another example is in the sale of a business. Imagine you are a CPA with a tax practice in a small town and you wish to sell your business. A buyer is willing to buy provided you agree not to practice in the town for a period of five years. The buyer is aware that your clients have a comfort level with you and would come to do business with you if you do the same work in a similar location. In each case, the primary purpose of the contracts was not to restrain trade. One was an employment contract and the other was a business sale. A court would most likely find these reasonable restraints in both contracts and would thus be enforceable. Typically, in employment contracts the restraints must be both reasonable and necessary to be upheld in court.

Withdrawal Before Performance/Partial Illegality

Another exception to the harshness of the "in pari delicto" rule leaving the parties where they stand is where one party offers to withdraw from the illegal agreement before performance. The law obviously wants to encourage that kind of behavior. Still another exception is where a contract has an illegal portion of it that can be deleted from the agreement. This usually happens when a new statute is enacted and an existing contract has several terms to it. For example, I contract to spray your farmland using DDT and a special weed killer. Use of DDT becomes illegal by statute. We are able to delete the portion of the contract using DDT, but can continue to enforce the agreement that calls for the weed killer.

There are some areas of public policy where the courts must look at the cases on an ad hoc basis and determine whether or not the contracts or clauses are enforceable. Some of those issues are discussed below.

Exculpatory Clauses/ Unconscionability

A contract that excuses one party from liability for future negligence, recklessness or intentional acts has an exculpatory clause (also referred to as a legal disclaimer). Generally, courts will not enforce contracts with such clauses as one cannot be excused from future tort liability. For example, you park your car at a valet parking garage where the attendant gives you a ticket that says, "ABC Parking is not liable for any damage done to your car for any reason. Owner assumes all responsibility for any damage that may possibly occur." One of the attendants recklessly damages your automobile while parking it. Despite the clause, it is likely that ABC Parking will be liable for damages as the exculpatory clause is unenforceable as a violation against public policy. Most would contend it is unreasonable.

The courts will not enforce a contract that is grossly unfair or unduly harsh. In certain situations, one party may have an unequal bargaining position giving him or her the ability to take advantage of another. Clauses that call for exorbitant penalties if a party is slightly late in a contract have been found to be unconscionable. For example, charging a $100 per day late fee on a bill of $500 would probably found to be unconscionable as well as possibly usurious. The UCC allows the court to scrutinize contracts to determine fairness in a commercial setting and determine if agreements are unduly harsh for one of the parties.

Capacity

Another fundamental element that must be met in contracting in addition to mutual assent, consideration and legality is capacity of the parties. Both parties must be legally capable to contract. In general this means that the parties must understand the subject matter of the contract and be competent to contract. Summarized below are parties who may be unable or limited in their ability to contract.

Minors

A minor is someone who has not reached majority age. This is defined in most states as being less than eighteen years old. Minors in general have the right to contract. Think of all the times that as a fifteen-year-old you went to a fast food restaurant and purchased food. While minors can contract, they are afforded exceptional protection in that they can disaffirm most contracts. They have the right to get back all consideration they originally tendered by voiding the contract and returning the consideration they have received. For example, Junior Smith, a 16 year old minor, purchases a stereo from XYZ Stereos for a price of $300. He uses the device for a couple of months, chooses to return it and is entitled to his entire $300 back. He can get all of the money he tendered despite the fact the stereo is depreciated and possibly damaged. As you might imagine, contracting with minors can be risky.

Minors are liable for necessities they purchase to the extent that they must pay a reasonable value for those necessities they have received. Necessities include such things as food, clothing, medical care, education and similar goods and services. Providers of such items must have actually provided the items in order to recover under this quasi-contractual theory. For example, a minor contracts to purchase a $200 suit of clothes but disaffirms before she receives the suit. In this case the minor will receive the full purchase price back because the suit has not yet been provided. However, if the suit is provided and the seller is able to prove the suit is a necessity then the minor will be liable for the reasonable value of the suit, which may be less than $200.

States have statutes that limit minor's ability to disaffirm certain contracts they have made. For instance, in some states a minor cannot disaffirm an insurance contract or a checking account. Court ordered contracts must be adhered to by minors as well. A classic example of a court ordered contract is where minors have liability is child support.

A contract with a minor can be ratified only after the minor reaches majority age or a reasonable time thereafter. For example, a 17 year old minor purchases a stereo for $800 on an installment plan. He continues to pay for the stereo after his 18th birthday. His actions ratify the contract. He also could have expressly ratified the contract by notifying the seller of the stereo. Ratification can take place after majority age by keeping the consideration on the contract and continuing to use it. It can also take place by selling the consideration to another party after reaching majority age. In all cases, ratification takes place after majority age.

Incompetents

Individuals who are under court appointed guardianship, where the court has appointed someone to manage the individual's affairs cannot contract. The agreements they make are void. In some cases, providers of necessities are able to recover a reasonable value of goods or services they have provided a person under guardianship under the theory of quasi-contract.

An individual who has a mental illness or defect who cannot understand the subject matter of a contract has the option of voidability in contracts he or she makes. Part of the ability to assent to a contract requires that the party understand what is being agreed to. Despite having the option to void contracts, an individual suffering from mental illness or a mental defect is liable under quasi-contract for a reasonable value of necessities furnished to him or her.

Intoxication

An agreement that one makes while intoxicated and unable to understand the subject matter of a contract is voidable. However, slight intoxication does not destroy one's capacity to contract. Voluntary intoxication tends to make it difficult to void a contract if the non-intoxicated party had no reason to suspect the other party was intoxicated. One does not have the right to take advantage of another's intoxication. Such a contract is voidable by the intoxicated party. In all cases of intoxication, the party who voids must do so promptly and return consideration that he or she received or the right to disaffirm will be lost. Additionally, intoxicated persons are liable for necessities received while intoxicated.

Chapter 11

Third Party and Form

"A verbal contract isn't worth the paper it's printed on." – Samuel Goldwyn

When we think of a contract, typically we think of two parties who have agreed to terms of one kind or another with each party directly benefiting and being detrimented. I agree to purchase your car for $5000. I receive the benefit of the car and am detrimented in having to pay you $5000, with you being benefited and detrimented in a similar way. We are in privity of contract, meaning we are both parties to the contract.

Assignment of Rights

There are events in some contracts that cause performance to be transferred to beyond the two parties involved. Use the above example and imagine that you owe a friend $4900 that you are late in paying. You ask me to pay the friend directly to remove your liability for the debt, and you persuade your friend to accept the payment. You are assigning your rights to the $5000. Your friend has now acquired rights to the consideration in our contract. An assignment is a voluntary transfer of contractual rights to a third party, not involved in the contract.

The individual transferring the rights, you in the above example, is the assignor. The individual receiving the rights, your friend who is owed the $4900, is the assignee. The individual who must perform in the contract, the one who owes $5000 for the car (me), is the obligor.

The general rules of assignments are as follows:

Consideration for the assignment is not required. An assignment can be a gift.

If an assignment is provided for consideration, the assignment cannot be revoked without the consent of the assignee. In the earlier example since you owed your friend $4900 and that debt is being relieved you could only revoke the assignment if your friend agreed.

A gratuitous assignment (one where no consideration is provided) is revocable.

Writing is not necessary for an assignment unless it falls within the statute of frauds (discussed later in the chapter).

An assignment cannot increase the duty, risk or burden of the obligor.

Most contractual rights can be assigned though some are not assignable. Duties that are highly personal in nature and rights that are expressly prohibited by contract terms cannot be assigned. Moreover, assignment of certain rights (like the right to vote in a public election) are prohibited by law and cannot be assigned.

Generally one cannot assign future rights.

The assignee stands in the shoes of the assignor and can bring action against the obligor if the obligor does not perform.

The obligor can claim any defense against performing the assignment that he or she could have claimed against the assignor. For example, if the assignor committed fraud, duress etc. against the obligor, the obligor could plead those defenses in not performing the contract. The obligor can also claim a setoff or counter claim against the assignor arising out of a separate claim as long as the action occurred prior to the assignment.

The assignor is bound by any express warranties made to the assignee regarding the assignment.

The assignor is also bound by implied warranties of law in the assignment. They include that the rights being assigned exist, that the assignor will do nothing to impair the assignment, that any writing held as proof of the right is genuine, and that the assignor has no knowledge of anything that might impair the assignment.

Third Party Beneficiary Contracts

Some contracts are made for the benefit of others. Life insurance contracts are an example of such. You pay Farmers Insurance $500 per year in a $100,000 term life insurance policy. You and Farmers are the parties to the contract. Your spouse is the intended beneficiary. Should you die, Farmers must pay your spouse the $100,000. Because your spouse is the intended beneficiary, she has rights in the contract and if Farmers does not perform she will be able to sue the company and collect. The contract was made on your spouse's behalf.

When a contract is made for another as a gift, the intended beneficiary is called the donee beneficiary. When a contract is made for another as a condition of a loan, the intended beneficiary is called the creditor beneficiary. For example, imagine you are a small business owner who seeks a million dollar loan for her business. The bank realizes that you are the one who makes the business run and in the event of your untimely death the bank may not be repaid. The loan terms require that you take out a million dollar life insurance policy during the life of the loan with the bank named as a beneficiary. Thus the bank is a creditor beneficiary.

An incidental beneficiary has no such rights. An incidental beneficiary is someone who happens to be lucky and receives a benefit as a result of being in the right place at the right time. For example, you own an undeveloped one-acre plot in a blighted area of your city. Your city contracts to build a new stadium next to your property. This causes your plot to increase substantially in value. The stadium developer defaults and the city decides not to pursue the stadium and the value of your lot drops. You have no rights in this issue. You would be unsuccessful in suing the developer or the city because you are an incidental beneficiary.

Delegation of Duties

Earlier we discussed the idea of rights in a contract being assignable. Duties in a contract cannot be assigned, but many can be delegated to another party. If I have an obligation to deliver 10 tons of sand to your business on Saturday, I can delegate that duty to perform to someone else. I remain liable to you for that performance and you can look to me or the party performing the delegated duty for performance. The delegator (the party delegating the duty) remains liable to the obligee (the person receiving the performance) in a delegation of duty.

Certain types of duties cannot be delegated. If the duties are highly personal in nature or the duties are expressly non-delegable by contract or by law, they cannot be delegated. For example, Luciano Pavarotti cannot delegate his duty to sing an opera at Flint Center in Cupertino to his friend, Guido. The singing of the opera is personal in nature. Public school teachers are prohibited by law to delegate the teaching of their classes to others by law and by contract.

A novation takes place when a third party takes the place of one of the contracting parties in a contract, and the new party assumes all performance of the contract while the substituted party is relieved of liability. For example, you contract with Joanne to deliver 10 tons of sugar per month to her candy plant for a price of $3,000 per month for one year. After three months you persuade ABC Sugar Refiners to take over the contract and Joanne is willing to relieve you of the contract. You are the delegator and are relieved of any liability in this novation.

Statute of Frauds

We discussed the premise that many contracts do not have to be in writing to be enforceable. There are some contracts that the courts will not enforce if they are not in writing. This idea originally came about in England in the 17th century when the statute to prevent frauds and perjuries in contracting was first enacted. Certain contracts were deemed to be so important with such risk to the parties that evidence of the agreement had to be in writing in order for the courts to act on them.

Now, all states have enacted a statute of frauds which requires written evidence of a contract in order to have a court enforce the agreement. If a contract falls within the statute of frauds, it requires a writing for enforceability. If a contract falls outside the statute of frauds a writing is not required for enforceability. The contracts that generally fall within the statute of frauds in most states are summarized below.

Land Interests

The sale of real property requires a writing in order for the court to enforce the agreement. Real property is defined as land or anything affixed permanently to the land. So buildings, permanent fixtures and trees are considered real property.

Suretyship

Answering for the duty of another falls within the statute of frauds. Suretyship works like this:

You contract to provide plumbing on a commercial project for a general contractor and agree to furnish all required parts before getting paid. This means you have to purchase plumbing products and install them. You need credit from a plumbing supply house in order to purchase the products. The supply house is only willing to extend credit to you if someone else will cover the bill if you cannot pay. You call a friend who is willing to be secondarily liable on the contract with the supply house. You purchase the products but do not pay the supply house and the supply house looks to your friend for payment. Because your friend is secondarily liable, meaning the supply house looks to you for payment first, written evidence of the contract will be required in order for the supply house to force your friend to pay.

Additionally, your friend cannot personally benefit in guaranteeing payment on the contract, otherwise it falls outside the statute of frauds. So if your friend was the general contractor on the project and guaranteeing your performance helped ensure that the job will be finished on time, then it would fall outside the statute of frauds and no writing would be required for enforceability.

For suretyship to fall within the statute of frauds it requires secondary liability (not primary liability where they look to both parties for payment), and a lack of benefit by the guarantor. This lack of benefit for the guarantor is referred to as the leading object rule meaning that the leading object or main purpose of the suretyship must not be for the benefit of the party who is guaranteeing the performance.

Personal Liability of an Executor/Administrator

When an individual dies and has made a will, he or she appoints an executor or executrix (man or woman) to settle the estate after the death. If the individual dies without a will the court appoints an administrator or administratrix to settle the estate. On occasion, the executor/trix, administrator/trix will promise a party who is owed money by the decedent that he or she will personally cover the debt if the estate does not have the funds to provide payment. In order to be enforceable, this promise must be in writing. Note, this is similar to the suretyship provision.

One Year Provision

Contracts that take longer than one year from agreement to execution require a writing for enforceability. For example, I agree to rent a space at a county fair from the County of Santa Clara on September 1, 2003 for the period of October 10-17, 2004. The rental period is only seven days, but the contract is agreed to over a year before it ends. The contract falls within the statute of frauds.

If there is the slightest possibility that the contract can be finished within twelve months, then it does not fall within the statute of frauds. You agree to employ someone for the rest of her life. Because that individual might not live over a year, the contract falls outside the statute of frauds.

Marriage Promises

When one party promises consideration to another for marriage a writing is required for enforceability. For example, you promise Helen that in exchange for marrying you that you will pay for her tuition to finish college. This promise falls within the statute of frauds. If you and Helen marry and you do not pay her tuition she will only be able to get the agreement enforced if she has a written evidence of the agreement from you.

Do not confuse this with a bilateral promise to marry where both parties agree to marry with no specific consideration promised. Those promises do not fall within the statute of frauds.

Sale of Goods

The UCC provides that the sale of goods of $500 or more require a writing for enforceability.

General Issues Involving the Statute of Frauds

There are other areas that are covered by the statute of frauds that vary from state to state. Moreover, there are some special rules and exceptions involving the statute of frauds and the sale of goods that are covered in your text. Make sure you cover those rules and understand how they work.

To comply with the statute of frauds requirement the writing does not need to be formal. The writing must specify the parties involved in the contract, specify the subject matter and essential terms of the contract with reasonable certainty, and be signed by the party against whom enforcement is sought. There can be open terms, there can be only one signature and there can be a series of writings that taken together show the objective intent of the contract.

Recognize that while a writing is not required of many contracts, it is still a good idea to have written agreements in many business settings.

Parol Evidence Rule

Some contracts are said to be integrated. An integrated contract is one where the writings are agreed to by both parties as being evidence of the complete agreement. Nothing outside of the terms and conditions written in the agreement are considered to be part of the contract. Moreover, the parties are not allowed to introduce oral or written evidence that is inconsistent with the written agreement that are not part of the contract. For example, you and I negotiate for an extended period of time for the purchase of a large networked computer system. The total price is $6 million. We have traded ideas for several days before agreeing to the price and a 12 month warranty. At various times we discussed a 24 month warranty, an 18 month warranty, a twelve month warranty and a 6 month warranty during the negotiations. The final written contract states 12 months. After the contract is completed I cannot introduce evidence that we agreed on a 6 month warranty. That term contradicts those of the contract. The parol evidence rule will not permit me to enter that "earlier" agreement into evidence. The contract stands as it is written.

Of course, if we agree during the performance of the contract to change terms, or if there is evidence of fraud, duress, lack of capacity or the like, then that evidence is admissible.

Interpretation of Contracts

There are certain standards of interpretation in contracts that the courts follow to resolve differences and ambiguities:

In a preprinted agreement, typed words have precedence over the preprinted terms and handwritten terms have precedence over both.

Ordinary words are interpreted by their ordinary meanings and technical words are interpreted by their technical meanings.

Ambiguities in the contract are construed against the party who drafted the ambiguity.

Parties in the same trade will have terms of the trade construed as part of the trade or however the terms are used in a course of dealing.

A writing or series of writings is interpreted as a whole writing interpreting terms that promote the objective or principal intent of the contract.

Chapter 12

Performance and Remedies

"A lean compromise is better than a fat lawsuit" – Italian Proverb

The reasonable expectation for performance in contracts is complete performance. Complete performance occurs when a party to a contract renders exactly what was promised in the agreement. Anything less than complete performance may be grounds for a breach of contract. Less than perfect or complete performance can take two forms: substantial performance or inferior performance.

Substantial performance is slightly less than complete performance. A minor breach to the contract has occurred, but the primary purpose of the contract is intact. For example, I agree to paint your house white with brown trim for a price of $1500. I paint the house as specified but fail to paint the trim on a door and a window. In this case the deviation is minor and if we went to court over the dispute I might be awarded $1350 for the job instead of the $1500 if the damages were shown to be $150. The main purpose of the contract has not been defeated.

A material breach occurs when inferior performance has been rendered by one of the parties and the primary purpose of the contract has been defeated. For example, a tile contractor contracts to lay a specific type of white porcelain tile in your kitchen. He lays green ceramic tile instead. Ceramic tile is of lesser quality than porcelain and the color is clearly wrong. This is a material breach of the contract. You are now discharged from the contract and may require removal of the ceramic tile. You may employ another tile contractor to do the job correctly as well.

The difference between a material and a minor breach depends upon the contract and its terms. There are no clear rules as to determine specifically when a minor breach becomes a material breach. As a general rule, intentional breaches of a contract are held to be material. Moreover, an intentional breach flies in the face of good faith and fair dealing in any contract. Contracts where the terms spell out a material breach, late performance where time is of the essence and quantitatively and qualitatively serious performance flaws tend to be seen as material by the courts.

Conditions of Contracts

A contract condition is an event that affects a party's duty to perform in a contract. There are several types of contractual conditions summarized below.

Condition Precedent

A condition precedent is an event that is uncertain that must occur in order for one of the parties in a contract to perform. For example, I agree to purchase your house for $400,000 conditioned upon my ability to get 8%, fixed rate, 30 year financing. If I am able to secure such financing the sale will go through, if I am not able to secure such financing then the sale is off.

Concurrent Conditions

Concurrent conditions take place at the same time during contract performance. Generally, the law assumes that contracts have concurrent conditions in the absence of terms dictating anything different. For example, when you purchase a cup of coffee at Starbucks, you pay for the coffee as you receive your drink. The conditions are concurrent.

Condition Subsequent

A condition subsequent is an event that discharges a duty of performance. For example, on occasion you might purchase an item and have the right to return it without paying for it for a certain period of time. You are discharged after performance has occurred.

Express and Implied Conditions

An express condition is one that is explicitly stated in a contract. One type of an express condition is personal satisfaction. This means that the party receiving performance must subjectively (in his or her own mind), be satisfied with the performance. For instance, I agree to have a professional photographer take my picture for the price of $400 and the photographer guarantees me personal satisfaction. The picture is taken and everyone who sees it believes it is a wonderful likeness of me. However, I do not like it. I am not satisfied. Most reasonable people contend that I am being unreasonable in my objections. I may be unreasonable but I am honest in my objections. I will not have to pay for the photo. Objective satisfaction takes place in business and can be expressed in a contract. A typical objective satisfaction condition occurs in the construction business where a building will be accepted when an engineering certificate is signed. Upon the happening of that event the building owner will have to pay the contractor.

Implied conditions can be implied in fact and implied in law. An implied in fact condition is a condition that both parties have inferred from one another in a contract and are part of the agreement. I agree to paint your house any color you choose for a price of $1500. It is implied in fact that you will notify me of the color.

An implied in law condition (also know as a constructive condition) is a condition that is imposed by law. This happens when one party performs fully in a contract before the other party performs at all. For example, a tailor contracts to sew a dress for you for the price of $500, but there is no mention of when and how payment must be made. When the tailor performs and delivers the dress, you are bound to pay the tailor at that point despite there being no mention as to terms of payment. The law imposes (constructively) conditions on both parties.

Discharge

Having discussed performance and conditions, the next step is to consider discharge in a contract. How does one complete a contract or be excused from performing in a contract? There are several ways that can happen.

Perhaps the best way to be discharged from a contract is by fully performing it. Once a party has fulfilled his duties in a contract, he or she is fully discharged and owes no additional performance. A tender of performance is where one party offers the other party in a contract to fully perform in a contract. If the receiving party refuses the performance then the party tendering is excused from performance.

As stated earlier, one party is discharged if the other party materially breaches a contract. This is a discharge by breach.

On occasion one party will provide substantial performance but less than perfect performance. The receiving party may accept the performance and seek damages to be set at the amount of non-performance.

If one party prevents another party from performing, the prevented party is discharged. The prevention of performance constitutes a material breach. For example, I hire you to do some plumbing on a large commercial project of mine where you will be paid at the end of the project. I persuade the plumbing supply house not to issue you credit, which makes it impossible for you to do the job. My actions have prevented you from performing and you are thus discharged.

If one of the parties intentionally, fraudulently, materially alters a written contract, the non-breaching party is discharged under the contract. This is another example of acting in bad faith.

Both parties can be discharged by agreement. Parties to a contract can agree to mutually rescind a contract or they can choose to substitute a new contract for the old and in both cases will be discharged from the original contract. We discussed novation earlier where one party can substitute another party in a contract and be discharged, provided all three parties involved agree.

An accord and satisfaction can substitute for a duty in a contract where both parties agree to provide different consideration during the course of a contract. For example, you owe me $200 for the purchase of my computer system last month. We agree that you can trim the trees in my yard in lieu of the debt. The agreement is the accord and the satisfaction will take place when you trim those trees in my yard.

A party can be discharged by operation of law. Bankruptcy will discharge an individual of debts owed under a contract, and the statute of limitations may prevent a party from using the court to help collect a debt that has been outstanding too long. If the subject matter of the contract becomes illegal, both parties are discharged. For example, you own a farm and contract with a pesticide company to spray 10 gallons of DDT on your crops every month for a year. The use of DDT is outlawed after three months. You are liable for payment for the three month's worth of spraying, but both parties are discharged from thereon.

There are some relatively unique ways parties can be discharged. One is by frustration of purpose, where if events occur in such a way that a contract cannot be performed, both parties are discharged. For example, you contract to stay in a hotel in Florida for a period of one week in September, but a hurricane comes through that requires the town be evacuated before you arrive and during the period of your planned stay. The purpose of the contract has been frustrated.

Commercial impracticability is a rare situation in a contract where if unforeseen circumstances or unjust hardship occurs during the contract, the parties can be discharged. The event cannot be caused by one of the parties of the contract and normal business risks like supplier strikes and shortages are not considered to be causes of commercially impracticability. Subjective impossibility should not be confused with commercial impracticability as an excuse for non-performance in a contract. For example, if your company contracts to do a $1million construction job that you find out will cost you $1.4 million because you bid poorly, your company will not be excused from performance. Your company took a risk and did poorly, it is not grounds for discharge.

Objective impossibility occurs when an event occurs that makes a contract impossible to perform. For example, Tiger Woods contracts to play golf with two golf fans on December 1 for a price of

$20,000, but breaks his leg on November 29 and cannot play. This is objective impossibility. The fans can get their money back and Woods will not be required to play.

Remedies

When a party encounters a breach by the other party in a contract, the non-breaching party has a right to a remedy under law. The courts allow the party that has suffered from lack of performance to recover damages of some sort.

The most common remedy in contract breaches is monetary damages. Losses that are foreseeable and can be determined with reasonable certainty are generally awarded in cases involving contract breach. There are several different types of monetary damages that can be awarded by a court:

Compensatory Damages

Compensatory damages are monetary damages awarded to the non-breaching party in a contract that theoretically put the injured party into as good a position as if the contract had not been breached. For example, imagine you are a retailer and have contracted with XYZ Toy Distributors to purchase 10,000 of the newest Star Wars dolls at a price of $7 each. XYZ breaches the contract and it costs you $10 each to purchase the dolls from another supplier. Your loss is $30,000 (10,000 dolls X $3 per doll) and your compensatory damages would be that amount in this instance. Any expenses that are saved must be considered as well. So if you were going to have to pay shipping with XYZ of $1000 and the new supplier does not charge for shipping, you would only receive $29,000 in compensatory damages.

Incidental and Consequential Damages

Incidental damages are those damages that arise directly from the breach of contract. Consequential damages are those damages that are not directly attributable to the breach but are a foreseeable result of the breach. In order to collect consequential damages the breaching party must know or should have known that the damages that were suffered would or could occur.

An example of incidental damages is shown in an employment contract. Imagine you have been hired to work as the manufacturing manager of ABC Manufacturing for a period of one year at a salary of $8,000 per month. You are fired without cause after five months when there are still seven months remaining on your contract. First, you have a duty to mitigate damages, meaning you cannot let the clock run and plan on suing and collecting your $8,000 per month for the seven months remaining on your contract. You must act in good faith and minimize your damages - look for another job. You pay an employment agency $500 to help you find work, and incur $300 in telephone and car expense as part of the job search process. You will be able to collect an additional $800 in incidental damages. Take this example a bit further and imagine that you find another job at a rate of $7,000 per month after a one month job search. You have to give up a deposit on your apartment worth $1500 because you need to move and had a one year lease that you committed to when you began working for ABC. The damages would be classified as follows:

Compensatory - $8,000 for the one month off of work
                     6,000 for the lesser salary for six months
            $14,000 total

Incidental -	$800 job search expense
Consequential -	$1500 lost deposit

The consequential damages would only be available if the company was aware that the unjust firing would cause you to lose your lease. Consequential damages are not awarded very often and are limited under the UCC.

Reliance Damages

Reliance damages put the breached party into as good a position as he would have been had the contract not been performed. For example, you contract to rent a space from a lessor at a crafts fair for $1000 to sell some goods that you made in art class. You purchase some supplies costing $150 in order to sell those goods. The lessor defaults and you are unable to return the supplies you purchased. Your reliance damages are $150. Reliance damages are not to be confused with restitution, which is discussed below.

Liquidated Damages

Some refer to liquidated damages as "pre-arranged" damages. This is because both parties to the contract arrange for damages in advance of a possible breach. For example, ABC Distributing contracts with you to deliver 10,000 swim suits at a price of $8 each to your retail store by April 1 of the current year. You both agree that for every day that ABC is late in delivering the goods that ABC will lose $200 on the contract up to a maximum of 10 days ($2000). Your losses as a result of late performance might be overtime for workers to put the goods out on display, a wasted ad in a newspaper etc. Liquidated damages must bear a reasonable relationship to the actual losses the party would have incurred and will not be enforceable if they are a penalty.

Nominal Damages

In some cases there are minimal or no damages suffered in a contract breach. When a party pursues such an action in court nominal damages may be awarded. For instance, you contract to purchase 1000 Speedo swimsuits at a price of $8 each from ABC Distributing. ABC defaults and you are able to get XYZ Distributing to provide the 10,000 suits for $7 each. The cost of finding the other supplier comes to approximately $1000, so you can't prove you've lost anything. The court might award you $1 in nominal damages. In some cases you might also be awarded court costs.

Punitive Damages

Punitive damages are damages awarded beyond compensatory damages and are generally not available for contract breach. They are available when a tort has also been committed and behavior by the breaching party has been unconscionable, willful or malicious.

Equitable Remedies - Specific Performance

There are situations in a contract breach where monetary damages are not appropriate. In this case the injured party seeks equitable remedies. For example, you lease a commercial building for your business and you plan your move for July of the current year. You have new cards printed, you contract with service providers to get you up and running on the July date and are ready to move. The lessor decides he will not make the space available to you and repudiates the contract. You are not interested in money in this instance, your are interested in occupying the commercial space. Consequently, you will sue for specific performance. You will ask the court to order the lessor to make the space available to you.

Equitable Remedies - Injunction

In other situations getting an injunction, a court order that stops a party from performing may be appropriate. For example, you contract with a well known singer, Bruce Summerstein, to perform at your nightclub during March of the current year. A competitor offers Bruce more money to perform at her club during that time. You will not be able to force specific performance on Mr. Summerstein, but you can get an injunction that keeps him from performing for your competitor during that March period.

Reformation

Reformation is the process by which a court will rewrite or correct a contract in order to make it conform to the original intent of the parties. This can occur when there are clerical errors in a contract. The court will correct such errors with proof of the mistake.

Restitution and Rescission

When parties provide consideration in a contract and then a breach occurs, restitution is available to one or both parties depending on the circumstances. Restitution puts the parties in their original positions before performance was provided in the contract. For example, you agree to purchase a house for $300,000 and put up a deposit of $5,000 during the closing period of the sale. The seller decides he does not want to sell and you choose not to pursue the matter. Restitution of the $5,000 is available to you. In this case you are rescinding the contract. Rescission effectively undoes the contract. In restitution the party returns consideration that has been tendered to him or to her. It is available to an injured party in lieu of alternative damages to the breaching party who has provided consideration where unjust enrichment would otherwise occur and for a party who is unable to enforce a contract because of the statute of frauds.

Remedy Limitations

Generally, multiple remedies are available to injured parties in a contract provided the remedies are consistent with the damages suffered. For example, one can sue for incidental damages in addition to injunction or specific performance if such damages have been suffered.

In disaffirming a contract or dealing with a breach it is important to remember that the injured party must act in good faith. The injured party has a duty to mitigate damages in a contract breach. Losses cannot be allowed to pile up unreasonably if the injured party can limit them. In the case of dealing with disaffirmance of a contract due to fraud, misrepresentation, lack of capacity or similar issues, the injured party has duty to disaffirm within a reasonable period of time or rights may be lost. If the party injured by fraud or similar action affirms the contract by continuing to enjoy the benefits of the contract, or delays unreasonably in disaffirming the contract, the party has effectively affirmed the contract and loses the right of disaffirmance. Third party rights can also intervene causing a loss of power of avoidance.

In seeking the courts' help, the maxim stating "Ye who seek equity must do equity," is one for injured parties to consider.

Chapter 13

Sales and Lease Contracts

"A merchant that gains not, loseth" – *George Herbert*

In earlier chapters we introduced and discussed the use of the Uniform Commercial Code and its relation to sales as part of general contract law. This chapter focuses exclusively on sales and lease contracts and how they are governed by the code. There are some general concepts and terms regarding sales and the UCC that are summarized below:

Sale of Goods

A sale of goods takes place when there is a transfer of ownership of personal property for money, goods or services. Article 2 of the Code applies exclusively to the sale of goods, not real property, services, employment or the like. Thus, the first issue to recognize when evaluating a contract is whether or not it is an agreement that deals with goods and therefore falls under the code. If it does not deal with goods, then in most cases, common law will apply. A *mixed sale* is a sale that involves the provision of a service and a good in the same transaction. Article 2 of the UCC applies to mixed sales if the goods represent a majority of the transaction. Whether goods represent the predominant part of the transaction is considered on a case by case basis.

Leases

A lease of goods is a transfer of possession and use but not permanent ownership of goods that belong to another. Leasing has become a common way to acquire the use of personal property in recent years. Automobiles, computer equipment and similar items are leased regularly by businesses and consumers. Article 2A of the Code was added in recent years in order to ensure that leases would conform to sales contracts under the UCC. Article 2A effectively restates Article 2 of the Code except that it applies to leases of goods instead of sales of goods.

Specific Issues Addressed by the UCC

Definition of a Merchant

The Code defines a merchant as a person who deals in goods or by his occupation holds himself out as having knowledge or skill peculiar to one who has expertise or experience in dealing in goods. An individual who employs a merchant as a broker, an agent or other intermediary is considered a merchant in the eyes of the law as well. The merchant is held to a special standard of business conduct because he or she is seen as having a higher level of expertise in commercial transactions than that of a consumer.

Firm Offer

A firm offer under the Code is an offer in writing by a merchant expressing that the offer will be held open for a certain period of time. The offer must be in writing and signed by the offeror. A firm offer is not revocable by the merchant during the offer period. If no time period is stated during the offer period, then the offer will be terminated after a reasonable period of time up to a maximum period of three months.

Open Terms

Under the Code a contract for the sale or lease of goods is formed in any manner showing that the parties reached agreement. The Code allows for open terms in a contract and it will be held that a contract exists despite a lack of definiteness if it is found that the objective intent of both parties in the sale or lease of goods is to contract and there is reasonable basis for the court to grant an appropriate remedy.

The Code allows for open terms to be a part of a contract and specifies the following in specific situations:

Open Price Terms	If the parties have not agreed on a price, the court will determine a reasonable price at the time of delivery.
Open Payment	If the agreement lacks payment terms, payment is due at the time and place where the buyer receives the goods.
Open Delivery	If the contract is silent as to delivery, the buyer takes delivery at the sellers place of business.
Open Quantity	In general, if the parties do not specify quantities in a contract, the court has no basis for granting a remedy. The exception to this rule is output and requirement contracts. In output contracts the seller agrees to sell and the buyer agrees to buy all (or up to a maximum stated amount) that the seller produces. In requirements contracts the buyer contracts to purchase and the seller contracts to sell all (or up to a maximum stated amount) that the buyer requires. In both output and requirements contracts the code imposes a good faith limitation on both parties. Neither party can dramatically change quantities and exceed normal production during the contract period without first agreeing to the change.

Acceptance

Acceptance of an offer under the code allows for any "reasonable means under the circumstances" if the offeror does not specify a certain means of acceptance. Moreover, the "mirror image" rule seen in common law acceptances is not as stringent under the Code. The UCC holds that if the offeree indicates a definite acceptance of an offer, then a contract exists even if the offeree includes additional or different terms from those stated in the offer.

If both parties are non-merchants the additional terms are not part of the agreement. For example, you offer to sell your car for $3000 to Bill and Bill accepts your offer unequivocally and says he would like to have a tank of gas and new seat covers as part of the purchase price. The additional term is interpreted as a suggestion or proposal and you would not be required to comply with that term.

In contracts between merchants the additional terms automatically become part of the contract with the following exceptions:

The offeror objects to the new conditions within a reasonable period of time (usually 10 days).

The new or changed terms materially alter the contract.

The original offer expressly limits acceptances to the original terms of the offer.

Recognize that a merchant can make a conditional acceptance, which will not be construed as creating a contract if the acceptance communicates clearly that acceptance is conditioned upon the acceptance of additional terms. For example, ABC Supply offers to sell XYZ Retailer 1000 cabbage patch dolls at a price of $12 each totaling $12,000. XYZ accepts conditioned upon ABC providing the dolls along with special cabbage patch bracelets and allowing for payment three months after delivery as part of the contract for the price of $12,000. That would be a classic conditional acceptance and no contract would exist unless ABC consents to the new terms.

Modifications

Modifications to contracts can be made under the Code without both parties providing consideration if the change is agreed to and done in good faith. This is different from common law where modifications require both parties to give something up.

Rules of Construction

The Code provides rules of construction for interpreting contracts by setting precedence of which terms govern in an agreement. Course of performance, course of dealing, usage of trade and express terms are taken together when they do not contradict each other. If such construction is unfeasible then the order of priority is express terms, followed by course of performance, then course of dealing and finally usage of trade.

Unconscionability

If a contract can be construed to be so one sided or so monstrously extortionate that it would be unreasonable to enforce it, it will be construed to be unconscionable. The Code allows for the court to evaluate a contract or any clause in a contract and determine if the agreement was unconscionable at the time it was made. If the contract was unconscionable from the start then the courts can refuse to enforce the contract, enforce the parts of the contract that are not unconscionable, or limit the application of any unconscionable clauses to avoid unconscionability.

Chapter 14

Agency

"No man can serve two masters" – Proverb, adapted from the New Testament

Much of the work that we encounter in business is done through agency. When you go to a restaurant and order food from a waiter, you are dealing with an agent of the business. When you go to Macy's and purchase clothing, the sales clerk who helps you is an agent. In both of these examples the two businesses are getting work done through others. Agency is just that – getting work done through others. Agency law defines the relationship between the employer and employee. Agency can be non-work related as well. If you have ever had a friend sign you up for a club or a team, or had someone return books to the library on your behalf, you have had an agency relationship.

Agency involves three parties in the process of its activities. The principal is the individual who employs or appoints the agent to act on his or her behalf. The agent is the individual who acts for the principal. The third party is the individual or individuals who deal with the agent.

Employees and Independent Contractors

There are two basic types of agency relationships. The first is the employment relationship where the principal hires an agent as an employee. In the employer/employee relationship the employer is said to be able to exercise control over the employee. The employer can set working hours, terms of employment and determines to a great degree how the employee works. Most employer/employee relationships (but not all) are said to be *at will*. This means that the employee has the right to quit at any time and the employer has the right to fire or terminate the employee at any time. The employer is not allowed to fire someone in a discriminatory fashion and cannot abusively discharge an employee, but generally can terminate an employee without cause. While the *at will* agreement may seem harsh, it allows freedom for both parties to make a change quickly if needed.

Employers cannot terminate *at will* an employee who is on a fixed term contract. For example, you are hired as the superintendent of San Jose Schools and are given a three-year contract. It is expected that you will work there for the three years – if you don't you may be liable to the school district. And the district does not have the right to fire you without cause during the three-year period.

In addition to limits with fixed term contracts, many union agreements have a specific method of termination so an employer may be limited in that case as well. Finally, firms that have made promises as part of the employment bargain that they will not fire arbitrarily or promise to terminate using a specific method are limited in terminating employees. However, most contracts for employment are *at will* giving both employer and employee freedom.

The second type of agency relationship is that of the independent contractor. In this relationship the principal does not 'control' the agent. The agent is responsible for results only and is not under the control of the principal. This type of relationship typically has a time limit. The real estate agent sells your house and the relationship is over. The plumber fixes your pipes and the contract is executed.

Respondeat Superior

The employer has a great deal of potential liability for the acts of his or her employee under the doctrine of "respondeat superior." This means let the superior answer for the acts of the agent. The employer has this type of liability because the law has determined that society is best served by making the employer responsible for most acts done through an agent. It is thought that the employer will exercise care and caution if she is liable for acts of her agent. Moreover, it is thought that society is best served if an injured party can seek out the party with the deepest pockets in being compensated, and that usually points to the employer. Finally, the entrepreneur theory states that if a principal is going to benefit from the agency relationship, then she should incur the risk as well.

In general, we are not liable for the acts of independent contractors unless they do something we directed them to do. For example, if a large company like Hewlett Packard hires a driver as an employee to deliver parts to different HP sites and the company is not careful in screening the driver and he causes an accident on the job, HP will be held liable and be looked to for damages. On the other hand, if you hire a professional plumber to unclog your sink and he leaves the job briefly to purchase a missing part from a supply house and causes an accident where someone is injured; you will not be liable in that case. You do not control his actions as an employer does.

Capacity of the Agent

In general, almost anyone can be an agent. Minors can be agents. Newspapers all over the country have appointed minor agents, some as young as 10 or 11 years old, to act as their agents in delivering newspapers. Even individuals who are insane and lack capacity can act on another's behalf. However, principals are wise to exercise care and caution in appointing agents in that they can be liable for many of their acts.

Capacity of the Principal

In order to be a principal one must have capacity to appoint an agent. The relationship between principal and agent is consensual (meaning both parties agree to the relationship). In some states minors are not allowed to be principals, in others, minors may be principals but the agency is voidable by the minor.

Agency Types

Agency can take the form of special or general agency. A special agent is empowered to do a specific act or some specific tasks on behalf of the principal. For example, you decide to sell your house and hire a real estate broker to market and sell the property. The broker has been hired to do one specific act – sell your house. He or she is not empowered to do anything else for you. Additionally, there is a time limit to the relationship.

A general agent is empowered to conduct a series of transactions over time. The general manager of a department store who is empowered to hire and fire workers, order goods and the like is a general agent. He will partake in a number of different activities over time and has responsibility for more than one or a few specific acts.

Fiduciary Responsibility

Certain agents have a fiduciary responsibility to their principals. This relationship is one of binding trust between the parties and the agent has the duty to exercise the highest degree of loyalty and good faith in handling the principal's affairs. It is usually seen in independent contractor relationships such as attorney/client, real estate broker/client etc. If an independent contractor has been hired to act on behalf of the principal with third parties and can contract on behalf of the principal, then the contractor is an agent and has a fiduciary responsibility. If the contractor is not empowered to deal with third parties and cannot bind the principal to contracts then there is no fiduciary responsibility. An attorney has a fiduciary responsibility to her client. A gardener who is hired to cut a principal's lawn has no such duty.

Duties

Both the agent and principal owe duties to one another throughout the course of the agency relationship. The following is a summary of such duties:

Duties of Agent to Principal

> Duty of Loyalty and Good Faith
>
> Duty of Obedience
>
> Duty of Diligence
>
> Duty to Inform
>
> Duty to Account
>
> Fiduciary Duties – not to compete, avoid conflicts of interest, keep confidential information confidential, account for financial benefits

Duties of Principal to Agent

> Indemnification
>
> Reimbursement
>
> Compensation – unless it is a gratuitous agency

Termination

An agency relationship can be terminated in one of several ways. The following summarize the different types of termination of an agency agreement:

Agreement of the Parties

Fulfillment of Agency Purpose

Renunciation by the Agent

Lapse of Time

Operation of Law

    Change of law makes agency illegal

    Death of agent

    Insanity of either party

    Bankruptcy of agent if it affects agent's ability to perform

    Bankruptcy of principal

    Destruction of subject matter

    Loss of license or qualification of principal or agent

    Agent disloyalty

Liability for Contracts in Agency

Because the agent is appointed to act on behalf of the principal in various duties, it is reasonable to question what authority an agent has in situations and how that authority is granted. Authority comes in many different forms in an agency relationship and a principal is wise to understand how it is created.

Among the risks a principal takes in an agency relationship is when an agent exceeds his or her authority in dealing with third parties. In many cases, if the third party could reasonably believe that an agent had authority in representing the principal, the principal will be liable. The principal can then sue the agent, but that may be too little too late for the principal if the agent's pockets are not deep.

Actual Authority

Actual authority is granted by the principal to the agent by expressing specifically the acts an agent is empowered to do, or by implying what an agent may do. For example, you are hired by John Smith to market and sell his house. One year earlier you sold his previous house. The listing contract states you may put a sign out, advertise the address and price and solicit offers. These are examples of express authority. Implied authority is authority based on past dealings between the agent and third parties. When you sold Smith's house two years ago he gave you a key and allowed you to show the property when he wasn't home. He gives you the key again. The implication is that you may show the property again when he isn't home.

Ratification authority takes place when an agent exceeds his or her granted authority but the principal ratifies the act. When that occurs the principal ratifies, the entire act is ratified, not just the benefits of what occurred.

Apparent Authority

Apparent authority occurs when the principal creates the appearance to third parties that an agent has greater powers than he or she was granted. For example, you are the owner of a retail store and you hire a manager to take care of the normal daily business. In your industry it is not common to allow managers to purchase inventory and you have never granted permission to your manager to do so. You mention to a salesman in passing that you're very happy with the new manager and she is empowered to do "whatever it takes" to keep the store running. When the salesman calls on your manager, if she orders inventory you will probably be liable because the salesman reasonably believed your manager had more authority than you had actually granted her.

When terminating an agent, principals must be careful to not allow apparent authority to carry on with third parties. For example, you fire a general manager who had the power to order inventory. You do not notify your suppliers who have been used to dealing with your general manager on orders. If your general manager orders inventory from one of your suppliers after he is fired you will likely be liable under apparent authority.

Disclosed/Undisclosed Principals

There are situations where principals do not wish to be known that they are interested in a transaction. It is to their benefit to stay behind the scenes. For example, imagine that you are a well-known athlete who has made a lot of money over the past several years. You are interested in purchasing a vacation home in Lake Tahoe. The market is soft in Tahoe at this time. If the sellers become aware that you are interested in purchasing their property they may be disinclined to negotiate their price downward. Consequently, you hire an agent to represent you in the transaction and instruct the agent to act as though the purchase is on her behalf, with no mention of your involvement. You are an undisclosed principal.

In a dispute where an undisclosed principal is involved, the third party believes he is dealing with the agent as a principal. Consequently, the third party can sue the agent as well as the principal. As a general rule, both the principal and agent are liable to a harmed third party in an undisclosed agency.

A partially disclosed principal is one where the third party is aware there is a principal, but is unaware of the principal's identity. In general, the agent is personally liable in these cases along with the principal. There are situations however, where both the agent and principal agree that the principal will be exclusively liable should the third party suffer damages.

A disclosed principal is one where the third party is aware of the existence and identity of the principal. Generally, the agent is held harmless and the principal is liable on such agreements. There are exceptions in that if an agent intends to be bound on the contract he or she will be liable. The agent will also be liable if he or she leads the third party to believe that his or her capacity exceeds the actual capacity granted. The third party can sue either the principal or the agent, but cannot collect twice or double in a dispute.

Employment Issues

As stated earlier, most employment agreements are *at will* agreements which mean either party can terminate the contract at any time. State and federal law play a large part in employment contracts in terms of setting working conditions, minimum pay, immigration, citizenship and similar issues. Many states classify employees in two different categories. One category is *exempt*, meaning that the employer is not liable to pay the employee overtime if he or she works beyond a minimum number of hours in a day (usually 8) or a week (usually 40). This class of employee is generally considered to have a high skill level in the workplace, can work somewhat independently and is often classified as a "professional." This class of worker is salaried on a weekly, monthly or yearly basis. For example, most engineers, attorneys, purchasing agents, managers, certified public accountants and financial analysts are in the exempt category. Terms in an employment agreement for exempt workers will often have wording such as: *"As an exempt employee you are required to work the number of hours required to get the job done…You are required to devote your full energies, efforts and abilities in your employment unless your Employer expressly agrees otherwise"* setting an expectation of high commitment in the workplace.

The other category of worker is non-exempt, meaning workers in this category are entitled to overtime premium pay in the event that they work over a minimum number of hours (usually 8 in a given day and/or 40 hours in a given week). This class of worker is generally paid on an hourly basis. For example restaurant workers, certain production workers and clerical staff are usually *non-exempt*.

Many employment agreements have an arbitration clause that indicates that in the event of a dispute binding arbitration will be utilized to resolve the dispute. Additionally, the employment contract will often outline the dispute resolution procedure.

It is common in the high-technology and biotechnology industries for employees to sign a proprietary information agreement as part of the employment contract. This agreement clarifies that the employee cannot bring trade secrets to the current workplace from a previous job. Moreover the employee agrees that all information gotten from the present firm and a all work performed at the firm is proprietary – meaning it belongs to the firm and not the employee – and the employee does not own or have any rights to any intellectual property developed at the firm.

Multiple Choice

Chapter 1   **Law Overview and Legal History**

1. The system of travelling courts as a basis for providing laws comes from:

a) Roman Law System
b. Code of Hammurabi
c. Feudal Period
d. Mosaic Law

2. The idea that the king was chosen by God and should answer only to God is found in:

a. The king speaks ex cathedra
b. William the Conquerors Court
c. Charlemagnes Law
d. the divine right of kings

3. The civil law system seen in several European countries today is based on:

a. English law
b. Feudal law
c. Jewish Law
d. Roman Law

4. The American system of law is based primarily on:

a. English Common Law
b. Roman Law
c. Feudal Law
d. Mosaic Code

5. When an authoritative body promulgates law, it:

a. interprets law
b. ignores the law
c. puts forth law
d. repeals the law

Chapter 2   **Legal Philosophy**

1. The United States passing anti-discrimination laws in the 20th century is an example of adhering to:

    a. the individual ethic
    b. the moral ethic
    c. the societal ethic
    d. the laissez faire ethic

2. Early in U.S. history the idea of "a deal is a deal" and the government staying out of the transaction is an example of:

    a. laissez faire philosophy
    b. the societal ethic
    c. common law system
    d. divine or natural law

3. The philosophy of divine or natural law is first ascribed to:

    a. Roscoe Pound
    b. Immanuel Kant
    c. Ronald Reagan
    d. Aristotle

4. Using the law to move society toward certain behavior follows which philosophy?

    a. Historical School
    b. Social Engineering
    c. Divine or Natural Law
    d. Economic School

5. Judging an action in the light of what would happen if everyone in society made the same decision and followed it out can be ascribed to:

    a. Aristotle - Natural Law
    b. Volcker - Economic School
    c. Kant - Categorical Imperative
    d. The Golden Rule

Chapter 3 **Classifications of Law**

1. Traffic laws are an example of what type of laws?

a. Substantive/Private/Criminal
b. Substantive/Public/Criminal
c. Procedural/Public/Civil
d. Procedural/Private/Criminal

2. Sue Baroo suing Chic N. Haus for a contract breach is an example of what type of laws?

a. Substantive/Private/Civil
b. Substantive/Public/Criminal
c. Procedural/Public/Civil
d. Procedural/Private/Criminal

3. The Miranda decision requiring that the police read rights to an arrested suspect is an example of:

a. Civil Law
b. Procedural Law
c. Codified Law
d. None of the above

4. A suit for monetary damages is a suit in:

a. Civil Court
b. Criminal Court
c. Equity Court
d. None of the above

5. An injunction is a:

a. Remedy at equity requiring the losing party to pay damages
b. Remedy at law requiring the losing party to pay damages
c. Remedy at equity requiring the losing party to cease or desist an action
d. Remedy at law requiring the losing party to go to jail

6. A preponderance of the evidence is to civil court as:

a. Monetary damages are to criminal court
b. Monetary damages are to civil court
c. Beyond a reasonable doubt is to criminal court
d. Imprisonment is to criminal court

7. The supreme law of the land is:

a. Federal Statutes
b. Federal Treaties
c. State Constitutions
d. U.S. Constitution

8. What do we call the individual who files a civil suit?

a. Federal Prosecutor
b. Plaintiff
c. Defendant
d. State Prosecutor

9. Legislative laws are called:

a. Case law
b. Common law
c. Statutes
d. Equitable remedies

10. What is a decision by a court of equity called?

a. Judgment
b. Decree
c. Maxim
d. Code

11. Criminal guilt must be proved:

a. by a preponderance of the evidence
b. without a doubt
c. beyond a reasonable doubt
d. by a legal majority of the evidence

12. Which of the following laws would take precedence over a state constitution?

a. federal common law
b. federal statute
c. state statute
d. a and b above

13. Federal common law would take precedence over:

a. the U.S. Constitution
b. federal statute
c. state statute
d. federal treaty

14. The defendant in a civil lawsuit:

a. initiated the lawsuit
b. is being sued
c. will appeal in all cases
d. none of the above

Chapter 4   Jurisdiction, Courts, Civil Procedure

1. If David, a resident of California, gets in a car accident with Lisa, a resident of Oregon and Lisa sues David for $150,000. The case will be heard in:

a. U.S. District Court
b. State Trial Court
c. Federal Appeals Court
d. Either a or b above

2. An example of a specialized court at the federal level would be:

a. U.S. District Court
b. State Traffic Court
c. Bankruptcy Court
d. State Superior Court

3. In rem jurisdiction refers to jurisdiction over

a. a person
b. a city or a state
c. property or a thing
d. federal property

4. A civil dispute between a Sunnyvale, CA manufacturer and a San Jose retail shop in the amount of $100,000 would be held in:

a. U.S. District Court
b. State Traffic Court
c. Bankruptcy Court
d. State Superior Court

5. Sergio is a potential juror on a civil case involving a former employee who is suing Intel Corp. for wrongful discharge He is asked by one of the attorneys if he has any opinion about the case or the parties involved. Sergio says he knows that most fired employees are whiners and losers and moreover; Sergio says he owns 200 shares of Intel stock. It is likely Sergio will be excused from serving based on:

a. peremptory challenge
b. inconvenience
c. challenge for cause
d. Sergio cannot be excused from jury duty

6. Which of the following terms do NOT belong in the discovery phase of the trial?

a. deposition
b. pleadings
c. interrogatories
d. requests for admissions

7. Benny is a potential juror on a civil case. The defendant's attorney notices Benny wearing an American flag on his lapel. The attorney is afraid Benny is conservative and will not be sympathetic to his client's case. Benny is dismissed without reason. This jury dismissal for Benny is termed:

a. challenge for cause
b. constitutional challenge
c. peremptory challenge
d. judicial challenge

8. A motion requesting that the judge rule contrary to the jury's decision in a case is called:

a. directed verdict
b. summary judgment
c. judgment on the pleadings
d. judgment notwithstanding the verdict

9. The preliminary examination of jurors is termed:

a. voire dire
b. peremptory challenge
c. challenge for cause
d. interrogatory

10. A motion made before the case goes to trial but after the discovery phase of the trial is called:

a. motion for a summary judgment
b. motion for a judgment on the pleadings
c. demurrer
d. motion for a default judgment

11. Which of the following would fall under federal exclusive jurisdiction?

a. a suit between two citizens of Idaho regarding a breach of contract
b. a suit between a citizen of Ohio and a citizen of Nevada in the amount of $120,000
c. a bankruptcy suit
d. a federal tax issue
e. c and d above

Chapter 5   Constitutional and Administrative Law

1. Which of the following rights are guaranteed in the constitution?

a. right to employment
b. freedom of speech
c. right to medical care
d. freedom of religion
e. b and d above

2. An example of government fiscal power is:

a. the Food and Drug Agency
b. excise taxes levied on citizens
c. regulation of firearms
d. free speech rights

3. An administrative agency has the power to:

a. investigate
b. make rules and regulations
c. issue sanctions
d. all of the above

4. Laws that do not comply with the U.S. Constitution:

a. can be enforced under states rights
b. have validity in federal matters only
c. are enforceable during natural disasters
d. none of the above

5. An advertisement of a product would be considered

a. protected to a lesser degree than individual speech
b. commercial speech
c. both a and b
d. neither a nor b

6. An administrative agency makes law in the form of:

a. adjudication
b. rules and regulations
c. enforcement
d. legislation

7. The "fourth branch of government" refers to:

a. the constitution
b. the military
c. administrative agencies
d. the house of representatives

8. The contract clause in the constitution:

a. allows a state to change private contracts as needed
b. prevents a state from changing contracts after they have been made
c. requires state approval of contracts between and among states
d. none of the above

9. The U.S. Constitution is preempted by:

a. state constitutions
b. federal statutes
c. state common law
d. administrative agency decisions
e. none of the above

10. The commerce clause in the constitution:

a. is a broad source of power held by the federal government to regulate the economy
b. allows states to regulate intrastate commerce with no interference from the federal government
c. includes the right to bear arms
d. is part of the first amendment

11. The Food and Drug Administration, a federal agency,

a. can suspend constitutional rights in certain regulatory situations
b. must adhere to the constitution in all matters
c. must adhere to its enabling statute
d. b and c, not a

Chapter 6   Torts

1. Juan is walking out of class and Ben angrily knocks Juan's hat off his head. Ben has committed:

a. assault
b. battery
c. conversion
d. defamation

2. Holding a knife to someone's neck and threatening to cut him or her and then releasing the knife is:

a. assault
b. battery
c. neither assault nor battery because there is no injury
d. false imprisonment

3. Spreading negative, false rumors about someone's business or business interests is:

a. defamation
b. libel
c. slander
d. disparagement

4. The Alviso Times reports that Lotta Love, a prominent city coucil member of Milpitas, has not paid her property taxes for three years. It turns out that the story is untrue, Lotta's sister, Little has not paid her property taxes. Lotta sues the Times for defamation. It is clear that the Times were not acting with malice in the story and an interviewed city official gave the wrong information. Lotta will

a. win, because the Times was negligent in its research
b. win, because Lotta is a public figure
c. lose, because Lotta is a public figure and there was no actual malice
d. lose, because of the statute of frauds

5. In determining professional negligence, a licensed real estate agent will be held to:

a. a reasonable person who is knowledgeable about real estate
b. a reasonable real estate agent working in the local industry
c. a person the agent's age and education
d. a newly licensed real estate agent

6. The difference between trespass to personal property and conversion is:

a. one relates to real property and one relates to personal property
b. one has civil liability and one has criminal liability
c. the measure of damages
d. one is intentional and one is a negligence tort

7. The term 'intent' in relation to a tort relates to:

a. an evil or hostile motive
b. desiring the consequences of one's act
c. criminal negligence
d. none of the above

8. Which of the following could be considered a battery?

a. J touches B's shoulder to get his attention while waiting in line
b. A, a flight steward kisses C, a passenger during a long overnight flight, while C sleeps,
c. a physician performs a breast examination on a patient
d. B laughs loudly at R who is standing 10 feet away

9. Professor Guggenheim is mixing combustible chemicals in his home driveway and causes a small explosion. His neighbor's window is shattered and the fence is damaged. He may:

a. be liable for personal property trespass
b. be liable under strict liability
c. be liable for violation of a criminal statute
d. be liable under negligence per se
e. b, c and d

10. Art regularly burns garbage at his industrial plant. He does not violate any local laws, but the neighboring business gets a great deal of his smoke and soot, causing a fall off in customer traffic. Art may be liable for:

a. conversion
b. trespass to real property
c. nuisance
d. contract infringement

11. Storeowners can sometimes have a problem with detaining shoplifters because:

a. a false accusation and detainment often results in a criminal battery charge
b. detaining a suspected shoplifter can result in a false imprisonment suit
c. stores have no right to detain suspected shoplifters
d. shoplifters are not read their Miranda rights

Chapter 7   Contracts

1. Contracts are governed primarily by

a. federal statutory law
b. federal common law
c. state common law
d. state statutory law

2. An example of a contract that falls under the UCC is:

a. a contract to purchase a computer
b. an employment contract
c. a service contract to prepare taxes
d. a contract to purchase a patent

3. A contract allowing one or both of the parties to withdraw and cancel the agreement is:

a. void
b. voidable
c. statutory
d. unenforceable

4. A contract where both parties exchange promises and make a commitment is:

a. unilateral
b. unenforceable
c. statutory
d. bilateral

5. Unjust enrichment is a concept recognized in:

a. implied contracts
b. quasi-contract
c. unilateral contracts
d. charitable subscriptions

6. A(n)_____contract is one that has no effect because it is missing an essential element.

a. void
b. voidable
c. bilateral
d. implied

7. Which of the following is not an essential element of all contracts?

a. mutual assent
b. writing
c. consideration
d. legality

8. Which of the following is not an essential element of all contracts?

a. mutual assent
b. equity
c. capacity of both parties
d. legality

9. The term for not performing in a contract without an excuse is:

a. misnomer
b. fraud
c. breach
d. implied

10. Juan promises to give $75,000 to a non-profit art gallery over the next five years. Based on that the gallery takes out a long-term lease on a building and starts several new projects. Juan pays the first year, but nothing thereafter. It is likely that the art gallery will be able to collect the money based on the concept of:

a. unjust enrichment
b. charitable subscription
c. promissory estoppel
d. certainty of offer

Chapter 8   Offer, Acceptance, Invalid Assent

1. The three requisites of a valid offer are: manifest an intent to contract, communication and:

a. a writing
b. definite and certain
c. revocation
d. mirror image

2. Which of the following offers cannot be revoked?

a. firm offer under the code
b. option contract
c. unilateral contract where substantial beginning has occurred
d. all of the above

3. Art makes an offer to Juan that is valid for 30 days. On the 10th day a federal law is passed making the subject matter of the offer illegal. The status of the offer:

a. remains on the table for 20 more days
b. terminated
c. is extended only until the first of the month by statute
d. none of the above

4. In a counteroffer, the offeree:

a. rejects an offer and makes an offer
b. accepts the offer
c. rejects an offer and withdraws
d. remains the offeree

5. An exception to the mirror image rule is:

a. in service contracts where price has been agreed
b. in contracts for intangibles
c. in the code under the battle of the forms
d. in a contingent counteroffer

6. An offer to sell goods will terminate:

a. at the date specified by the offeror
b. after a reasonable time if no termination date is stated
c. when the offeree stipulates the date
d. a and b above

7. Acceptance is effective upon_____. Rejection is effective upon____.

a. receipt, dispatch
b. dispatch, receipt
c. communication, counteroffer
d. a and c above

8. An auction with reserve:

a. requires that the highest offer be taken
b. does not allow the auctioneer to withdraw the article
c. allows the auctioneer to withdraw the article if bidding isn't high enough
d. reserves space for certain bidders

9. Physical duress renders a contract:

a. voidable
b. executory
c. bilateral
d. void

10. Mental duress renders a contract:

a. voidable
b. executory
c. bilateral
d. void

11. Jaime tells Anna that the computer he is selling her has never been used; just taken out of the box once. In fact the computer was used daily for 6 months. Jaime will be liable for:

a. undue influence
b. fraud in the execution
c. mental duress
d. fraud in the inducement

12. In the above example, what rights will Anna have?

a. keep the computer if she likes it, even if Jaime wants to void the contract
b. void the contract and get her money back
c. void the contract and sue Jaime in tort
d. all of the above

Chapter 9   **Consideration**

1. Manny's mother offers Manny $50 if he promises to stop cracking his knuckles and burping in public for one month. If Manny agrees this is:

a. not a valid contract because Manny shouldn't do those things anyway
b. a valid contract because Manny is giving up a legal right
c. a gratuitous promise
d. an illusory promise

2. If ABC is going to deliver goods later to XYZ than originally contracted, XYZ can demand something in return.

a. False, both are merchants and have no right to additional consideration
b. False, late delivery is a material breach which rescinds the contract
c. True, XYZ has a right to reasonable consideration
d. True, ABC originally had an illusory promise in the contract

3. Generally, common law requires _____ _____ when modifying a contract.

a. bilateral consideration
b. unilateral consideration
c. gratuitous promises
d. illusory promises

4. Under the UCC, modifying a contract where only one party provides consideration is:

a. unacceptable whether the parties agree or not
b. acceptable only in service agreements
c. acceptable if the parties act in good faith
d. only acceptable between two merchants

5. If John promises to purchase all of the soft drinks he might need for his business in 2003 and 2004 from ABC Beverage:

a. ABC is bound to supply all of John's soft drink needs regardless of what they might be
b. John has made an illusory promise
c. This contract is a conditional contract
d. This contract falls outside of the UCC

6. A promise that induces reliance which will create an injustice if the promise is not performed is:

a. conditional contract
b. quasi-contract
c. promissory estoppel
d. requirements contract

Chapter 10   Legality and Capacity

1. An attorney's license is:

a. revenue raising
b. regulatory
c. not necessary to practice law
d. none of the above

2. John gets a life insurance contract where his wife will receive money in the event of John's death. John jokingly refers to the contract as a "death bet." This is (a/an):

a. gambling agreement
b. usurious
c. risk shifting agreement
d. wagering agreement

3. If Abby sells her hair salon to Larry and Larry requires a term that does not allow Abby to open another hair salon in the country for 12 years, chances are this term will be:

a. unenforceable as unreasonable
b. enforceable if both parties agree
c. enforceable, but for only 10 years
d. unenforceable because restraints of business are wholly illegal

4. Terms in an agreement where one party has substantial bargaining position over the other and appears to take advantage of that position can give rise to:

a. regulatory issues of trade restraint
b. revenue issues of trade restraint
c. unconscionability
d. exculpatory clauses

5. A term that excuses a party from future negligence is called:

a. usury clause
b. wagering clause
c. santa clause
d. exculpatory clause

6. "In pari delicto" means, and the court _____.

a. to each his own, enforces the agreement
b. at equal fault, leaves the parties where they stand
c. at equal fault, requires a bond before the hearing
d. at equal fault, and the court enforces the agreement.

7. Ed, a 17 year old minor, purchases nine compact discs from Moon Records for a price of $81. Ed listens to them for a couple of months and returns the items demanding a full refund.

a. Moon must pay because Ed is a minor
b. Ed will be liable because the cd's are a necessity
c. Ed's parents are liable
d. Moon will be successful in suing Ed on breach of contract

8. A minor can ratify a contract:

a. anytime before reaching majority age
b. only after reaching majority age
c. anytime before or after reaching majority age
d. only before reaching majority age

9. Slight intoxication by party in a contract:

a. destroys one's capacity to contract
b. makes the agreement void
c. does not destroy one's capacity to contract
d. makes the agreement voidable by the non-intoxicated party.

Chapter 11   Third Party Contracts and Form

1. John is owed $100 by Annie. John assigns his right to the $100 to Art. Who is the obligor?

a. John
b. Annie
c. Art
d. Beavis

2. An express warranty in an assignment is one that is:

a. implied in law
b. implied in fact
c. spoken or written by the assignor
d. implied by the assignee

3. Homer takes out a $250,000 life insurance contract with the bank as a beneficiary in order to get a small business loan. The bank is a(n):

a. donee beneficiary
b. incidental beneficiary
c. creditor beneficiary
d. safe harbor

4. Kurt Favre, an all-pro quarterback, contracts to run a football camp for three days in the summer. He decides to go fishing instead and delegates the duty to his brother Jaime. This is:

a. an invalid delegation, personal duties
b. a valid delegation, Jaime is liable
c. a valid novation despite the fact that the football campers never agreed to the change
d. none of the above

5. Lucy agrees to pay Ricky's tuition at college if Ricky does not pay. Lucy receives no benefit from Ricky. This contract:

a. falls outside of the statute of frauds
b. is an integrated contract
c. must comply with the parol evidence rule
d. falls within the statute of frauds

6. Venus agrees to work for Serena as a trainer for a period of two years. Both agree to all the terms of the contract and integrate it. Venus finds out that Serena was fraudulent. Venus may:

a. not introduce fraud because this contract is integrated
b. introduce fraud despite the integration
c. only introduce the fraud if it came after the date of the agreement
d. introduce fraud if Serena agrees to it.

Chapter 12   **Performance and Remedies**

1. Larry agrees to purchase Linda's car contingent on his receiving a job offer by the end of the week. This is an example of:

a. condition subsequent
b. implied in fact condition
c. condition precedent
d. concurrent condition

2. Lonnie needs to have his watch repaired and takes it to the neighborhood jeweler. He tells the jeweler the problem, and then they discuss the baseball season. No terms of the contract are discussed. Lonnie leaving his watch at the jewelers is an example of:

a. condition subsequent
b. implied in fact condition
c. condition precedent
d. concurrent condition

3. Pablo contracts with Annie to decorate her living room and guarantees personal satisfaction. If Pablo does a wonderful job but Annie dislikes it:

a. Pablo is protected because of reasonability
b. Pablo is not protected because of the subjective standard here
c. If Pablo can get a licensed designer to agree that the job is reasonable, Annie has no recourse
d. None of the above

4. A contract to deliver swimming apparel by May 1 states "time is of the essence" as one of its terms. The clothing is delivered six weeks late on June 15. It is likely that:

a. a material breach has occurred
b. this is a clear case of substantial performance
c. a novation has occurred here
d. none of the above

5. A substituted duty in a contract and the discharge of a prior obligation is termed:

a. novation
b. bankruptcy
c. accord and satisfaction
d. subjective impossibility

6. A novation involves:

a. substitution of consideration
b. substitution of parties
c. bankruptcy
d. accord and satisfaction

7. Which of the following ways can a party NOT be discharged from performing on a contract?

a. objective impossibility
b. frustration of purpose
c. subjective impossibility
d. subsequent illegality

8. Jonathan contracts to provide catering services for the Smith wedding. He hires Martha Bakers to bake the cake at a price of $2000. Two days before the wedding Martha Bakers backs out and Jonathan finds Stewart Bakers and contracts with Stewart to bake the cake at a price of $2900. Jonathan sues Martha for $900. He is seeking:

a. nominal damages
b. liquidated damages
c. compensatory damages
d. restitution

9. Jonathan contracts to provide catering services for the Smith wedding. He hires Martha Bakers to bake the cake at a price of $2000. Two days before the wedding Martha Bakers backs out and Jonathan finds Stewart Bakers and contracts with Stewart to bake the cake at a price of $1900. Jonathan sues Martha and is awarded $1. He received:

a. nominal damages
b. liquidated damages
c. compensatory damages
d. restitution

10. Jonathan contracts to provide catering services for the Smith wedding. He hires Martha Bakers to bake the cake at a price of $2000. He pays Martha $400 as a deposit. Two weeks before the wedding Martha Bakers backs out and Jonathan requests his $400 deposit back. He is seeking:

a. nominal damages
b. liquidated damages
c. compensatory damages
d. restitution

11. The Smiths hire Simon Paul to sing at their daughters wedding at a price of $5000. Their hated neighbors, the Jones, entice Simon to sing at their 20th wedding anniversary on the same day at the same time for a price of $6000. Simon cannot sing at both so he breaks his contract with the Smiths. The Smiths wish to keep Simon from singing at the Jones'. They will sue for:

a. specific performance
b. injunction
c. liquidated damages
d. punitive damages

Chapter 13   **Sales and Lease Contracts**

1. Elaine purchases a small ranch. The contract for real property will most likely governed by:

a. the UCC
b. common law
c. administrative law
d. none of the above

2. Sun Stereo makes a signed written offer to sell 200 of its "Premium 230" brand speakers to San Jose Theatre at a price of $150 each. The offer is silent as to termination date. The offer will be:

a. revoked
b. open until acceptance
c. open until acceptance or three months whichever comes first
d. construed as an invitation to negotiate

3. Leonard contracts to lease a new Ford Taurus for a price of $299 per month for 36 months. the contract will fall under:

a. common law
b. the UCC
c. administrative law
d. patend law

4. A sequence of previous conduct between parties that establishes a basis for interpreting agreements is defined as:

a. usage of trade
b. a requirements contract
c. a course of dealing
d. merchant

5. If there is no specified place of delivery in a contract the code provides for delivery to be:

a. at the buyers dock
b. negotiated
c. seller's place of business
d. none of the above

6. If no payment terms have been indicated in a contract, the code provides for payment:

a. after all warranty periods
b. upon title change at delivery
c. within 90 days of acceptance
d. to be negotiated

7. The allowance for lack of a mirror image in an acceptance is seen in:

a. common law contracts
b. administrative contracts
c. UCC contracts
d. no contracts

8. A firm offer under the code:

a. may be revoked
b. may not be revoked
c. need not be in writing
d. none of the above

9. A lease contract for goods:

a. is intangible and therefore falls under common law
b. falls under the UCC
c. cannot be contracted for between states
d. none of the above

10. Modification to a contract under the code requires:

a. consideration and agreement by both parties
b. agreement and good faith by both parties
c. consideration but no agreement
d. agreement but no good faith

Chapter 14   **Agency**

1. Anna works at Super Foods. She mistakenly tells a customer that premium chicken breasts are being sold for 29 cents per pound instead of $2.29 per pound. The customer purchases 30 pounds of the chicken breasts. Later in the day the store owner finds out about Anna's mistake. The owner will:

a. be able to rescind the contract with the customer - lack of express authority on Anna's part.
b. have to live with the contract because Anna is an agent with enough authority in this case.
c. ratify her unauthorized acts
d. none of the above

2. Juan gives his colleague Edwina $2 to purchase a cup of coffee. Juan is the ___ Edwina is___.

a. agent/principal
b. third party/agent
c. principal/agent
d. manager/subordinate

3. Joe owns a carpet business. He hires workers on a daily basis to lay carpet. The workers provide their own tools and drive their own cars to the jobs where company trucks deliver the carpet. Joe tells them where they will work, how much time each project will take, when to show up and when to take lunch and quit for the day. This is most likely a/an:

a. independent contractor relationship
b. employer/employee relationship
c. power of attornye relationship
d. none of the above

4. One of the key terms in determining employer/employee vs independent contractor is:

a. control by the principal
b. subjective intent of the parties
c. agreement by the parties
d. ratification by the third party

5. A third party has _____ to verify the authority of a purported agent.

a. no duty
b. a duty
c. no recourse
d. none of the above

6. Paul works for ABC as a purchasing agent. A salesman from XYZ who does a lot of business with ABC through Paul gives Paul a $250 gift certificate for Christmas. Paul:

a. may keep the gift and not tell ABC
b. may keep the gift and not tell ABC because its Christmas
c. must inform ABC and turn the gift over to the company
d. must inform ABC but may keep the gift in any event

7. Maria works full time as a CPA for Numbers Inc. While doing taxes for one of Number's clients she suggests that the client come to her directly on the weekends where she does taxes on the side.

a. this is proper in competitive business
b. while this is questionable, it is acceptable in business
c. she is breaching her agency duties in this instance
d. she has no obligation to Numbers Inc.

8. A disclosed principal causes liability to fall on:

a. himself or herself
b. the agent exclusively
c. the third party
d. all of the above

9. An agent misrepresents a fact to a principal's client. The agent is acting entirely within the scope of his agency. The principal is:

a. liable to third party
b. held harmless
c. liable only if the agent admits the misrepresentation
d. none of the above

10. Which of the following ways do NOT end an agency agreement?

a. time lapse
b. revocation
c. renunciation
d. affirmation

Key Terms   **Chapter 1**   Name_____

Law

Norms

Sanctions

Promulgate

Code

Common Law System

Civil Law System

Divine Right of Kings

Feudalism

Summons

Felon

Summons

Precedent

Laissez Faire

Stare Decisis

Exercises   **Chapter 1**   Name_____

1. Explain the origins of civil and common law systems.

_____
_____
_____
_____

2. Define the term "laissez faire" and explain how it is (was) applied in the making and carrying out of law in the United States.

_____
_____
_____
_____

3. What does the term ethical behavior mean to you? Do business law and ethics go together? Why or why not?

_____
_____
_____
_____

4. List three reasons for having law in a society that were not discussed in the Guide.

_____
_____
_____
_____

5. Why do you think that the idea of the "Divine Right of Kings" came into being in certain societies?

_____
_____
_____
_____

Key Terms   **Chapter 2**   Name_____

Laissez Faire

Individual Ethic

Societal Ethic

Divine/Natural Law

Social Engineering

Historical School of Jurisprudence

Economic School of Jurisprudence

Kohlberg's Theory of Moral Development

Kant's Categorical Imperative

Exercises   **Chapter 2**

1. A company you own stock in chooses to support the following in a given year:

A non-profit theatre with a donation of $50,000
The United Way with a donation of $100,000
$25,000 to a non-profit agency called Freedom of Choice that does pregnancy counseling and provides abortions
25,000 to a non-profit agency called Children's Saviors that does pregnancy counseling and is firmly anti-abortion in its principles

How do you feel about these choices? Write a short letter to the president of the company explaining how you feel and why you think what she did was right or wrong.

2. Discuss a company that you know has been socially responsible. What has it done and what is the effect? Compare that to a company that appears not to be socially responsible. What is the effect?

Key Terms　　　　**Chapter 3**　　　　Name_____

Public Law

Private Law

Substantive Law

Procedural Law

Civil Law

Criminal Law

Plaintiff

Defendant

U.S. Constitution

State Constitution

Federal Treaty

Executive Order

Statute

Administrative Agencies

Beyond a Reasonable Doubt

Preponderance of the Evidence

Equitable Remedies

Codified Law

Exercises   **Chapter 3**   Name_____

1. Give an example of several different equitable remedies available in civil law.

_____

_____

_____

_____

2. What are the reasons for not having private parties initiate and try criminal cases?

_____

_____

_____

_____

3. Discuss and give examples of the differences between civil and criminal law.

_____

_____

_____

_____

4. If you sued the governor for a dog bite you received while visiting at his home, would the case fall under public or private law? Explain why.

_____

_____

_____

_____

5. Can a state constitution provide additional rights beyond the U.S. Constitution? Why or why not?

_____

_____

_____

_____

Exclusive Federal Jurisdiction

Concurrent Jurisdiction

Diversity Jurisdiction

Exclusive State Jurisdiction

In Personam Jurisdicition

In Rem Jurisdiction

Attachment

Venue

Minimum Contacts

Trial Courts - Federal

Trial Courts - State

Appeals Courts

U.S. Supreme Court

State Supreme Court

All terms associated with the chronology of a lawsuit

Key Terms   **Chapter 5**   Name_____

Separation of Power

Federalism

Checks and Balances

Federal Supremacy and Preemption

Judicial Review

Federal Commerce Power

Federal Fiscal Powers

Eminent Domain

Freedom of Speech

Corporate Speech

Rulemaking

Exercises   **Chapter 5**   Name_____

1. Consider a television or a radio advertisement and indicate how commercial speech is protected to a lesser degree than individual speech in our society.

_____

_____

_____

_____

2. What is the difference between substantive and procedural due process?

_____

_____

_____

_____

3. In your opinion, how far should freedom of speech go? Should advertisers be allowed to express opinions that disparage competition? Should satire be protected to the degree where it is crude or obscene in some opinions?

_____

_____

_____

_____

4. Several states have enacted statutes allowing for the medical use of marijuana. The federal government has (thus far) a clear policy against allowing cannabis clubs and the like to distribute the drug. Can the federal government overstep a state initiative? If so, under what authority?

_____

_____

_____

_____

5. What are the reasons that a court can review and set aside an administrative agency decision? Give an example of two ways that an agency decision might be overturned.

_____

_____

_____

_____

6. Why are administrative agencies referred to as the "fourth branch of government?"

_____

_____

_____

_____

7. Name two federal and one state administrative agency other than those mentioned in the Guide and explain their functions.

Key Terms **Chapter 7** Name_____

Contract

Uniform Commercial Code

Mutual Assent

Consideration

Legality

Capacity

Bilateral Contracts

Unilateral Contracts

Express Contracts

Implied Contracts

Valid Contracts

Void Agreements

Voidable Contracts

Unenforceable Contracts

Quasi-Contract

Promissory Estoppel

Charitable Subscriptions

1. What type of contract law would a sale of stereo equipment and a real estate lease fall under? What is the difference between the subject matter of both contracts?

    _____
    _____
    _____
    _____

2. Explain how contract law has changed in American society. What are the reasons for the change?

    _____
    _____
    _____
    _____

3. Identify the essential elements of a contract and explain each.

    _____
    _____
    _____
    _____

4. How are quasi-contract, promissory estoppel and charitable subscriptions related?

    _____
    _____
    _____
    _____

5. The Delta Party DeAnza Fraternity House has offered a $150 award to the first person to swim naked in the college pool between the hours of midnight and 5AM when the pool is closed. Chic N. Haus does the nude swim on November 1, and Sue Baroo does the nude swim on November 3. Sue comes to the frat house on November 4 to show the video, the frat says they will let her know when payment will be made. Chic comes and shows his video on November 6. The frat says they will let him know when payment will be made. Neither party is paid by November 30. Who should be paid and why?

    _____
    _____
    _____
    _____
    _____
    _____
    _____
    _____

6. The ability to drop a college course before the end of the term and receive a non-punitive 'W' grade has been described as a voidable contract. Do you agree? Why or why not?

Key Terms   **Chapter 8**   Name_____

Essentials of an Offer

Offer Revocation

Option Contract

Firm Offer

Rejection

Counteroffer

Destruction of Subject Matter

Time Lapse

Subsequent Illegality

Battle of the Forms

Authorized Means

Rules of Acceptance

Fraud in the Inducement

Fraud in the Execution

Mental Duress

Physical Duress

Undue Influence

Unilateral Mistake

Mutual Mistake

Exercises   Chapter 8

Name_____

1. List and explain the requisites of a valid offer.

_____
_____
_____
_____

2. List and explain the ways an offer can be terminated.

_____
_____
_____
_____

3. What are the exceptions to offeror revocation?

_____
_____
_____
_____

4. Lilac A. Rugg is auctioning without reserve several valuable art pieces from her gallery. The last item, a painting by Yanni entitled "Waxing the Car" receives no offers for ten minutes. Lilac pulls the painting off and the following week one of the patrons who attended the auction is threatening to sue Lilac for not selling the painting. Will Lilac be liable? Why or why not?

_____
_____
_____
_____

5. J.L. Breaker and Sons owned a building and land on First Street in San Jose, CA. It decided to sell the property by using a sealed, written bidding process. All potential bidders met the minimum qualifications for bidding. ABC submitted a bid for $1.2 million and XYZ submitted an alternative bid for $900,000 and/or $1 higher than the highest bid received. J.L. decided to sell the property to ABC after consulting with its attorneys. XYZ sued J.L. in a specific performance lawsuit arguing that the property should have been sold to them. Who should prevail here and why? Make sure you advance both sides of the argument.

_____
_____
_____
_____
_____
_____
_____
_____

Key Terms   **Chapter 9**   Name_____

Legal Detriment

Legal Benefit

Illusory Promise

Output Contracts

Requirement Contracts

Preexisting Public Obligation

Preexisting Contractual Obligation

Undisputed Debts

Disputed Debts

Accord and Satisfaction

Composition Agreements

Past Consideration

Moral Obligations

Promissory Estoppel

1. Explain the difference between modification of a contract at common law and modification under the code.

_____
_____
_____
_____

2. Explain the differences between a disputed and an undisputed debt.

_____
_____
_____
_____

3. Would an off-duty police officer who catches a criminal suspect in the city where he works be eligible for a reward offered for the criminal's capture? Why or why not?

_____
_____
_____
_____

4. Explain how a composition agreement works. Why would a creditor be willing to agree to one?

_____
_____
_____
_____

5. Explain how in the concept of quasi-contract that the requirement for consideration can be seen as being met.

_____
_____
_____
_____

6. Why should small business owners understand the concept of contract modification and settlement of disputed and undisputed debts?

_____
_____
_____
_____

7. Give an example of an accord and satisfaction other than that provided in the Guide.

Chapter 10   **Legality and Capacity**   Name_____

Key Terms

Licensing Statutes

Insurable Interest

Public Policy

Exculpatory Clause

In Pari Delicto

Majority Age

Minors

Disaffirmance

Ratification

Incompetency

Intoxication

Chapter 10   Exercises

1. Why are illegal bargains not called contracts?

_____

_____

_____

_____

2. Explain the difference between assumption of risk and an exculpatory clause.

_____

_____

_____

_____

3. What are the exceptions to the in pari delicto rule where courts will not help a party who is involved in an illegal agreement?

_____

_____

_____

_____

Key Terms   **Chapter 11**   Name_____

Assignment

Delegation

Obligor

Implied Warranties

Express Warranties

Novation

Creditor Beneficiary

Donee Beneficiary

Intended Beneficiary

Incidental Beneficiary

Statute of Frauds

Real Property

Suretyship

Leading Object Rule, Main Purpose Doctrine

Statute of Frauds - Sale of Goods

Parol Evidence Rule

Integrated Contract

Course of Dealing

Usage of Trade

1. Explain the concept of an assignment of rights in a contract. Give an example outside of those given in the Guide and the text.

_____
_____
_____
_____

2. Explain how a novation works. How does it differ from a delegation of duties?

_____
_____
_____
_____

3. Lillie is a tuba player. Jonathan is a conductor who badly needs a tuba player to complete his orchestra and perform for a group he contracted with earlier in the year. He persuades Lillie to become a part of the orchestra, but her tuba is at a pawn shop and she needs to sign a note payable stating she will pay $600 on or before July of the current year. The owner of the pawnshop tells Lillie that she must get someone to guarantee her payment. Jonathan agrees to become secondarily liable. Will the contract fall within the statute of frauds? If so why, if not why not?

_____
_____
_____
_____
_____
_____
_____
_____

4. ABC Manufacturing orally agreed to sell 200 metal boxes at a price of $2 each to XYZ Retailers. XYZ decided it could sell another 150 boxes more and called ABC orally requesting an increase in the contract to 350 boxes at a price of $2 each. ABC orally agreed but sent only 200 boxes. XYZ sues to force ABC to perform. Explain who will prevail and why.

_____
_____
_____
_____
_____
_____
_____
_____

5. Explain the possibility test in the statute of frauds.

_____

_____

_____

_____

_____

_____

_____

_____

6. John Brown signs a lease agreeing to rent a commercial space from XYZ Properties for a period of two years at a price of $24,000 total. The lease was a preprinted form and it stated that there are no pets allowed on the premises, in handwriting and initialed by both parties it was stated "one small dog okay." Three months into the lease XYZ discovered Brown was bringing his 20 pound shitzu dog to work and informed him that the lease was terminated because Brown violated the ban on pets. Will XYZ be successful in evicting Brown? Why or why not?

_____

_____

_____

_____

_____

_____

_____

_____

Discharge

Complete Performance

Substantial Performance

Material Breach

Express Condition

Implied Condition

Condition Precedent

Condition Subsequent

Concurrent Conditions

Substituted Contract

Accord and Satisfaction

Novation

Objective Impossibility

Subjective Impossibility

Frustration of Purpose

Commercial Impracticability

Bankruptcy

Compensatory Damages

Incidental Damages

Consequential Damages

Nominal Damages

Liquidated Damages

Reliance Damages

Restitution

Punitive Damages

Chapter 12 Continued   Name_____

Mitigation of Damages

Injunction

Specific Performance

Exercises   **Chapter 12**

1. Explain the different types of conditions that can be found in a contract and give an example
    not given in the Guide or the book.

    _____

    _____

    _____

    _____

    _____

    _____

    _____

    _____

    _____

2. Explain the differences between a material breach and a minor breach and how parties to a
    contract can disagree on the severity of a breach.

    _____

    _____

    _____

    _____

    _____

    _____

    _____

    _____

3. Explain the difference between objective and subjective impossibility.

    _____

    _____

    _____

    _____

    _____

    _____

    _____

4. What are liquidated damages, and why have them in a contract?

_____

_____

_____

_____

_____

_____

_____

_____

5. Explain the differences between compensatory and consequential damages.

_____

_____

_____

_____

_____

_____

_____

_____

_____

6. When would a party to a contract ask for restitution and why?

_____

_____

_____

_____

_____

_____

_____

_____

Key Terms   **Chapter 13**   Name_____

Goods

Lease

Sales Contracts

Merchant

Open Terms

Mirror Image

Non-merchants

Unconscionability

Rules of Construction

Exercises   **Chapter 13**

1. Explain the difference between a merchant and a non-merchant.

_____
_____
_____
_____

2. Chip Monk has been in the business of supplying paint to commercial companies for years. On 2/1 Polly Ester's Painting calls to purchase 100 gallons of Super Dry, Atrium White paint. Chip offers the 100 gallons at a price of $19 per gallon. Polly accepts. On 2/3 Polly sends the following letter confirming the deal. "As discussed and agreed, we hereby accept your offer of 100 gallons of Super Dry, Atrium White paint at a price of $19 per gallon. We also reserve the right to purchase up to 500 gallons more at the same price for twelve months from this date" (signed) Polly Ester. As of 2/21 Chip has not responded. Is there a contract? If so why, if not why not?

_____
_____
_____
_____
_____
_____
_____
_____
_____
_____
_____

Key Terms   **Chapter 14**   Name_____

Principal

Agent

Third Party

Independent Contractor

Employer/Employee

Express Authority

Implied Authority

Apparent Authority

Fiduciary

Disclosed Principal

Partially Disclosed Principal

Undisclosed Principal

Exercises   **Chapter 14**   Name_____

1. How does one create an agency?

_____

_____

_____

_____

2. Identify and the roles of the three parties are in an agency relationship.

_____

_____

_____

_____

3. Explain the difference between the employer/employee relationship and an independent contractor relationship in agency.

_____

_____

_____

_____

4. What does the term "at will" mean in an employer/employee relationship? ? Explain the advantages and disadvantages from the employer and employee perspective.

_____

_____

_____

_____

5. What are the duties of an agent toward a principal?

_____

_____

_____

_____

6. What are the duties of a principal toward an agent?

_____

_____

_____

_____

7. Explain the difference between actual authority and apparent authority.

_____
_____
_____
_____

8. Explain how the doctrine of "respondeat superior" works.

_____
_____
_____
_____

9. Jonathan is a design engineer for XYZ Robotics. He has worked with Harry's Machine Shop on the purchase of several machine parts for XYZ over the past year. He has a good relationship with Harry's Marketing Director, Mel Famey. At Christmas time Mel gives Jonathan a voucher for an all expense paid trip for two to Hawaii for 6 days paid for by Harry's Machine Shop. Is Jonathan permitted to accept the voucher and take the trip with his long-suffering wife, Nel? Why or why not?

_____
_____
_____
_____
_____
_____
_____
_____